Paganism for Beginners

An Essential Guide to Celtic, Norse, Slavic, Germanic, and Greek Pagan Practices and the Wheel of the Year

© Copyright 2024- All rights reserved.

The content contained within this book may not be reproduced, duplicated, or transmitted without direct written permission from the author or the publisher.

Under no circumstances will any blame or legal responsibility be held against the publisher, or author, for any damages, reparation, or monetary loss due to the information contained within this book, either directly or indirectly.

Legal Notice:

This book is copyright protected. It is only for personal use. You cannot amend, distribute, sell, use, quote, or paraphrase any part, or the content within this book, without the consent of the author or publisher.

Disclaimer Notice:

Please note the information contained within this document is for educational and entertainment purposes only. All effort has been executed to present accurate, up-to-date, reliable, and complete information. No warranties of any kind are declared or implied. Readers acknowledge that the author is not engaging in the rendering of legal, financial, medical, or professional advice. The content within this book has been derived from various sources. Please consult a licensed professional before attempting any techniques outlined in this book.

By reading this document, the reader agrees that under no circumstances is the author responsible for any losses, direct or indirect, that are incurred as a result of the use of the information contained within this document, including, but not limited to, errors, omissions, or inaccuracies.

Your Free Gift
(only available for a limited time)

Thanks for getting this book! If you want to learn more about various spirituality topics, then join Mari Silva's community and get a free guided meditation MP3 for awakening your third eye. This guided meditation mp3 is designed to open and strengthen ones third eye so you can experience a higher state of consciousness. Simply visit the link below the image to get started.

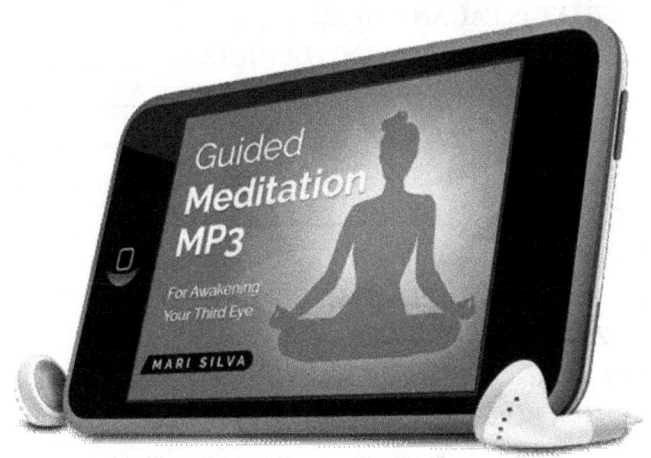

https://spiritualityspot.com/meditation

Table of Contents

INTRODUCTION 1
CHAPTER 1: WHAT IS PAGANISM? 3
CHAPTER 2: CELTIC PAGANISM AND DRUIDRY 14
CHAPTER 3: ASATRU: NORSE PAGANISM 25
CHAPTER 4: GERMANIC PAGANISM 38
CHAPTER 5: SLAVIC PAGANISM 49
CHAPTER 6: GREEK POLYTHEISM 60
CHAPTER 7: WICCA: A NEOPAGAN VIEW 71
CHAPTER 8: APPLYING YOUR PAGAN BELIEFS TO DAILY LIFE 83
APPENDIX: A-Z OF THE WHEEL OF THE YEAR 93
CONCLUSION 100
HERE'S ANOTHER BOOK BY MARI SILVA THAT YOU MIGHT LIKE 102
YOUR FREE GIFT (ONLY AVAILABLE FOR A LIMITED TIME) 103
REFERENCES 104

Introduction

What is Paganism? Is it an ancient religion or a modern practice? Does it still exist, and if so, what does it look like today? These are some questions asked about Paganism as interest in this long-standing tradition grows. Many are drawn to the idea of honoring nature and paying homage to deities generally forgotten by modern society. Yet with diverse cultures coming together to share their knowledge in the 21st century, it can be difficult to pinpoint what makes up pagan traditions.

From Wicca to Asatru and other practices which have influenced the world today, each has its beliefs making up its unique framework. Exploring Paganism brings many opportunities for self-reflection and understanding ancient cultures and modern practices, which continue to fascinate scholars everywhere. This book will help you explore the history and practice of these religions, demystifying them and providing practical advice to use Paganism in your everyday life.

Paganism is an umbrella term encompassing a wide variety of spiritual beliefs and practices, from Wicca and Druidry to Asatru and Pantheism. These faiths draw upon nature-based traditions that have been practiced since before recorded history. Each has unique rituals, symbols, practices, and ways of living harmoniously with the natural world.

This book provides an easy-to-understand overview of the various forms of Paganism so you can make a more informed decision about the right path for you. No matter what your knowledge level or experience with these practices, this book will give you everything to get started on your personal journey into Paganism. From understanding the core concepts and discovering their roots in human history to exploring rituals performed by neopagans, this book is a one-stop solution to Paganism.

This enlightening book delves deep into various pagan cultures, providing an intriguing look into each perspective. From the religious practices of Wicca to the philosophies and doctrines of Celtic-Druids, it guides readers through each path with interesting facts and stories. Furthermore, readers gain a greater insight into Asatru, Slavic, and Germanic pagan cultures with details about their respective rituals, holidays, superstitions, and spirituality. While this book is perfect for anyone wanting to learn about the pagan culture or comparing multiple cultures side-by-side, it's invaluable to experienced neopagans seeking more information about their and others' beliefs.

If you are only just starting your spiritual quest or looking for an introduction to the fascinating world of Paganism, then Paganism for Beginners is perfect. It contains everything from basic information about this ancient practice to detailed accounts of powerful rituals for deepening spiritual connection. It is presented in easy-to-follow language, so even beginners can get started quickly without fuss or complication. So, why wait? Embark on your journey now.

Chapter 1: What Is Paganism?

Intuitively, Paganism is often misconstrued as a foreign belief system for many people. This chapter explores in greater detail what Paganism entails, who pagans were, and how neopagans have interpreted these beliefs today. While old pagan concepts are regularly linked to nature and powerful deities, they also incorporated special festivals into their traditions and rituals, signifying the changing of seasons throughout the year. From morality and ethical behavior to worshipful spirituality, pagan principles taught valuable life lessons while encouraging people to connect to a deeper life purpose.

Pagans had rituals for the change of seasons.
https://pixabay.com/images/id-6982525/

Paganism

Paganism is an umbrella term to describe a wide range of spiritual and religious beliefs and practices based on pre-Christian traditions. It is typically polytheistic, meaning it involves worshiping multiple gods or goddesses. Paganism encompasses various modern and ancient belief systems, including those based on mythology, folklore, mysticism, and shamanism. These beliefs are animistic, meaning they view nature as alive and having its own spirit.

Paganism is based on a reverence for nature and a respect for the interconnectedness between all living things. It emphasizes personal responsibility, a balance between the physical and spiritual realms, respect for the wisdom of elders, and an openness to learning new things. Pagans believe divinity exists in all aspects of life, not only in deities but also in people, animals, objects, places, and plants.

Paganism has a rich history in many cultures worldwide. It can be seen in ancient Greek religion, Norse mythology, Celtic Paganism, Eastern European Slavic Paganism, Baltic Paganism, and Native American spirituality. It has been increasingly gaining traction in modern society as more people seek to reconnect with their ancestral roots through alternative spiritual practices.

Core Pagan beliefs include:

- Respect for nature and the environment
- Reverence for ancestors
- The interconnectedness of all life
- Balance between body, mind, and spirit
- Rituals to stay connected to the divine inner self
- Belief in magic
- Invocation of deities
- Use of symbolism as a means of communication with the divine
- Honoring male and female aspects of divinity (duotheism)
- A sense-related system rather than doctrine or dogma
- Living with intentionality rather than according to predetermined rules.

Pagans often practice their faith through ceremonies, such as handfasting (marriage ceremonies), sabbats (seasonal festivals), or esbats

(Moon rituals). Common tools used during these ceremonies include candles, herbs, stones, and other nature-based items. There is no one "right way" to practice Paganism as each individual has their own interpretation of what it means.

Pagan Beliefs

The pagans of old were polytheistic, believing in multiple gods and goddesses who inhabited the natural world. They believed these gods and goddesses were responsible for the various aspects of life, such as fertility, death, war, love, and justice. Pagans saw themselves as connected with their gods and goddesses through a shared relationship between the divine and earthly realms.

Pagans deeply respected the natural world, believing all parts of nature, trees, rivers, mountains, and animals, were alive with spiritual energy. This spiritual energy was seen as divine forces at work in the environment and among all living things. Pagans often held rituals and offerings at sacred sites throughout the year to honor these spiritual energies.

Additionally, some pagans believed in reincarnation or rebirth after death based on a person's actions during their lifetime. This belief in karma meant a person would be rewarded or punished depending on how they lived their life. Pagans held to several tenets of morality, such as honoring ancestors and respecting nature's cycles. For them, morality was essential for maintaining balance in the world.

Pagan Thoughts on Cosmology

Pagan thoughts on creation or cosmology vary greatly between cultures. However, all pagan traditions share a common theme: understanding the interconnectedness of all life and the cyclical nature of existence.

In Greek mythology, creation began with Chaos. This primordial void was filled with potentiality, and out of it, Gaia (Earth), Tartarus (the underworld), Eros (love), and Night were born. Gaia gave birth to Uranus (sky), and they created the Titans and Cyclopes, who would later help create humans from clay. This idea of a divine couple creating all there hugely influenced ancient Greek culture, forming the basis for much mythology and art.

The Norse Pantheon consists of various gods, including Odin and Thor, responsible for shaping their world at the creation. According to Norse cosmology, this world was created when Ymir, a giant, emerged from the icy waters of Ginnungagap. The gods constructed Midgard (Earth) from his body parts while his blood became oceans, his brain created clouds, and his skull formed the sky. Additionally, these gods are responsible for controlling fate which can be seen in the stories of Ragnarok, where they battle against giants to restore order to the universe.

In Wicca, creation is part of an eternal cycle reflected in their version of the Wheel of the Year – eight festivals that mark major events throughout each season, such as Samhain or Mabon. These celebrations are a reminder that life isn't linear but moves in circles and comes full circle each year; people experience death so that new life can be born again. Wicca views life as sacred energy which exists within everything, including plants, animals, and rocks, so they believe it's important to respect all forms of life by living in balance with nature rather than trying to control it through technology or science.

Druidism is another form of Paganism that focuses on spirituality over theology but still has a unique view on creation or cosmology. One example is in their version of the Triad, the three elements which make up existence: fire, water, and air, respectively, representing passion and inspiration (fire), creativity (water), and power (air). These three elements work together in harmony to create balance in life, and why Druids focus heavily on ritualistic practices like meditation or chanting to keep these energies aligned within them to understand their place in the universe better.

Pagan beliefs on creation or cosmology vary greatly between cultures but generally involve a deep respect for cycles within nature or connections between divine beings who shape reality at its inception. Whether it's Chaos birthing Gaia or Ymir being used as foundations for Midgard by Odin and Thor, there is always an understanding that life is fragile. Yet it is constantly evolving due to powerful forces beyond human understanding that must be balanced if peace and harmony within self and the environment are to exist.

Pagan Deities

Pagan deities are gods and goddesses, often polytheistic, who are worshipped by followers of Paganism. These deities often represent natural forces, such as the Sun and Moon, fertility, love, death, and destruction. These deities were widely revered in ancient societies stretching from Europe to Asia Minor.

Examples of pagan deities include:
- The Greek Pantheon of gods and goddesses such as Zeus, Athena, Apollo, and Aphrodite
- Norse gods such as Odin, Thor, and Freya
- Celtic gods such as Lugh and Brigid
- Druidic figures like Cerridwen
- Hindu gods like Shiva and Vishnu
- Ancient Egyptian deities like Isis and Horus
- Mesopotamian gods like Marduk and Ishtar
- Persian gods like Ahura, Mazda, and Mithras
- Slavic deities like Perun and Veles.

The ancient Greeks believed their Pantheon of twelve Olympian gods was responsible for all aspects of life, from the mundane to the extraordinary. They controlled the weather, determined political events, and inspired great deeds of courage on the battlefields.

The major Greek gods included:
- Zeus (king of the gods)
- Poseidon (god of the sea)
- Hades (god of the underworld)
- Hera (queen of Olympus)
- Apollo (god of light)
- Hermes (messenger god)
- Aphrodite (goddess of love)
- Hestia (goddess of hearth)
- Athena (goddess of wisdom)
- Ares (god of war)
- Demeter (goddess of the harvest)

- Artemis (goddess of hunting).

In Norse mythology, Odin is considered All-Father or "the Father God," while Thor is regarded as "the Thunderer" or god associated with thunderstorms. Other important Norse gods are Freyja, a fertility goddess associated with magic and nature worship, and Balder, known as "the shining god" due to his beauty and goodness. Freyja is associated with fertility rites and rituals involving seiðr, an old shamanistic magic practiced in Northern Europe long before Christianity took root there.

The Celts worshiped numerous gods, including Dian Cecht, known for healing and arts, and Lugh, a powerful Sun god associated with protection and justice. Ancestor spirits were held in high regard by Celtic pagans. Druids believed them to be messengers between this world and the otherworld, where they interacted with spirit guides or ancestors when seeking guidance. Brigid was a powerful goddess associated with fire, poetry, writing, and metalworking. Cernunnos was one of the most popular deities among druids and was associated with animals and fertility rites.

In Hinduism, there are numerous gods, all representing different aspects. The three major ones are Brahma, creator god; Vishnu, protector god; and Shiva, destroyer god. The trinity concept comes from these three major gods representing different creation, preservation, and destruction aspects. Many other Hindu Gods include:

- Ganesha, an elephant-headed lord who removes obstacles
- Kali, or Parvati, has multiple forms depending on the region in which she is being worshipped
- Lakshmi, goddess of wealth and abundance
- Saraswati, goddess of music, knowledge, art, and education

The Ancient Egyptians had many gods representing natural forces. Pharaohs were seen as manifestations of several divine entities: Horus, the god sky; Ra, the solar deity; Isis, the goddess of motherhood and magic; and Osiris, the god of death and the afterlife.

Slavic mythology has several primary gods, almost all represented by trees: Perun, the thunderstorm god; Jarilo, the springtime warrior god; Kupala, the water handmaiden god; Morana, the goddess of winter; Veles, the ruler of the underworld; Stribog, the wind lord; Dazbog, the Sun chariot driver; and Radegast, the lord of hospitality.

Importance of Nature

Nature was extremely important to pagans because it symbolized life's sacred and divine power. For pagans, nature was considered a living entity infused with spiritual energy. Therefore, by engaging in rituals and ceremonies within nature, they could tap into this spiritual power and use it to bring balance and harmony to their lives. Pagans regarded nature as an embodiment of the gods, goddesses, and other deities they worshiped. They held festivals throughout the year to honor the deities and pay homage to them in accordance with the natural cycles of life.

In addition to its spiritual significance for pagans, nature was a source of practical necessities, such as shelter, food, medicine, and clothing. By relying on nature for survival, pagans developed a deep respect for it, further contributing to its importance in their lives. Furthermore, pagan societies were largely agrarian-based, meaning their livelihoods were inextricably linked to nature's bounty. This connection strengthened their reverence for nature. Life cycles within nature (birth and death, growth and decay) were seen as symbols of transformation and renewal, serving as reminders that life is sacred and should be respected.

For example, in ancient Greece, the god Pan represented all aspects of nature through his connection to the woods and wilds. He was known as the god of fertility, shepherding, and even music, symbolizing how nature could provide sustenance and joy in equal measures. Nature was a source of healing and transformation for physical ailments or spiritual needs. The Oracle at Delphi drew upon natural elements, such as trees, water springs, and smoke from sacrificed animals, to gain insight into questions from the people who visited her from across Greece.

In Norse culture, nature was essential for understanding the world around them. The gods were often associated with certain elements of nature: Odin with wind (and battle), Thor with thunder (and protection), and Freya with fertility (and love). It linked deities to specific forces to explain why certain events happened in their lives. It helped them understand their environment, including unpredictable weather patterns, crop failures, and animal migrations.

The Wicca revere nature just as much. They believe it is connected to divine energy because it can give life and take it away if not respected properly. They hold rituals within natural settings like forests or meadows to honor the Earth's spirit while seeking guidance or protection. Wiccans use plants for spells and potions while celebrating important seasonal transitions throughout the year, connecting themselves spiritually with cycles like those in animals or plants.

Druids venerated trees and forests, believing they had healing powers and could communicate messages between themselves and their gods.

Overall, for these pagan cultures, nature provided an avenue toward understanding life's mysteries. By observing cycles within its vastness, they could draw connections between their faiths and everyday experiences more easily than modern-day religions typically allow. Nature was essential for survival during difficult times yet could provide hope for a better tomorrow, making it highly valued by these ancient societies.

Pagan Seasons and Festival

Pagans celebrated the seasons' cycles and the changing of light and dark throughout the year. The festivals, or holy days, usually began at sundown on the evening before and lasted for several days.

The Wheel of the Year was a cycle of eight festivals known as sabbats. Each marked an important time in nature's cycle and a celebration held during that time.

The sabbats were:

- Imbolc (Feb 1st)
- Ostara (spring equinox, around Mar 21st)
- Beltane (May 1st)
- Litha (summer solstice, around June 21st)
- Lammas (Aug 1st)
- Mabon (autumn equinox, around Sep 22nd)
- Samhain (Nov 1st)
- Yule (winter solstice, around Dec 21st)

During each season, pagans would come together to pay homage to their gods, thank Mother Nature for her bounty, and honor their ancestors gone before them.

At Imbolc, pagans celebrated the returning light after winter's long darkness. It is ushered in with fire ceremonies, honoring Brigid and lighting candles to signify her strength. They would chant blessings over seeds ready to be planted in the springtime soil, a symbolic way of honoring natural cycles.

Ostara marks the point where night and day are equal, known as balance or harmony between light and dark energies. It is traditionally celebrated with rituals involving eggs, a symbol of new life emerging from darkness. Many pagans gather in a circle and share stories about new beginnings while exchanging colored eggs filled with symbols of good fortune for each other.

At Mabon, which marks the autumn equinox when day turns into night again, pagans reflect on how far they have come since spring's first light. Harvest time has arrived, so ample opportunities exist for feasting on freshly gathered fruits and vegetables. It is common to bake bread using grains harvested during this period or make offerings out of apples, food associated with the fertility goddess Demeter who presides over Mabon celebrations.

Samhain marks the end of summer's growth and abundance and the start of winter's long chill. Pagans honor their ancestors by hosting rituals to help their spirits find peace on this plane rather than linger among mortals longer than necessary. People prepare foods like apple pies or roasted root vegetables as offerings to deceased loved ones. These offerings were thought to nourish souls when they needed it most during their journey beyond life's physical realm into the spirit world.

Neopaganism and Their Modern-Day Beliefs

Neopaganism is a modern spiritual movement that seeks to reconnect with pre-Christian, indigenous religions' ancient beliefs and practices. Neopagans attempt to revive and recreate the rituals, sacred sites, gods, and goddesses of the old world. They draw on many sources, including archaeological evidence, folk traditions, and historical texts. While many neopagan groups share some common core beliefs, each has unique customs and practices.

The term "neopagan" was first used in the 1950s by George Russell in his book "The Worship of Nature," which sought to bring together various strands of Paganism. Since then, neopaganism has taken on a life of its own as various groups have sought to revive the religion within their cultural context. Neopagans embrace several belief systems, including Wicca, Druidry, Shamanism, Celtic Reconstructionism, and Heathenism. They often practice seasonal or lunar celebrations known as sabbats or esbats to connect them with their ancestors and nature cycles. Many neopagans practice magic or spellwork for healing or protection, including herbal remedies or spells using the four elements (earth, air, fire, and water).

Neopagans adhere to an ethical code based on an awareness of the interconnectedness between people and all other creatures in nature (referred to as "the web of life"). Therefore, many neopagans seek to live in harmony with nature by avoiding activities like burning fossil fuels or over-hunting animals and engaging in conservation efforts like planting trees or cleaning beaches. Neopagans are highly concerned with environmental issues, such as global warming, pollution, and species extinction due to human activity.

Many neopagan groups emphasize community building. They believe it is important to come together regularly with friends and family to celebrate their faith and enjoy each other's company. These gatherings often involve feasting (including vegetarian dishes), storytelling, singing, dancing, drumming, painting, music, rituals, bonfires, and other activities celebrating life rather than a particular deity or event.

Whether modern-day neopagans hold similar beliefs and conduct similar customs or practices to their predecessors depends largely on what they consider "predecessors." For example, some contemporary Wiccans draw heavily from ancient Celtic tradition, while others draw from Norse Heathenism. Both differ from traditional Hinduism despite having some shared concepts, such as worshiping multiple deities or revering nature's cycles. Similarly, different branches of Druids have different beliefs about the afterlife; for instance, Hindus might not consider an afterlife (or have differing views, depending on sects).

Many contemporary neopagan practices align closely with those from ancient times.

- Honoring various gods and goddesses
- Sacred sites
- Ancestor veneration
- Seasonal festivals
- Oral traditions
- Natural objects used ritualistically
- Meditation
- Divination

- Herbal remedies
- Animal sacrifice
- Offerings
- Wild dancing
- Trances
- Drumming
- Chanting
- Poetry
- Mask making

Additionally, many neopagans focus heavily on specific deities, like Odin, Freya, Brigid, Athena, and Apollo. These gods often have specific associated characteristics celebrated through religious observances, characteristic behaviors, customary chants, mythologies, artwork, tales and stories, and symbols. Of course, even among those who practice similar beliefs, there are variations depending on individual preference, culture, society, and region. Therefore, when discussing similarities between modern-day neopagans, there will always be differences between individuals or groups. However, most neopagans honor certain core principles, such as respect for nature, honoring female and male gods, maintaining a connection with ancestors, and celebrating life and death cycles.

Chapter 2: Celtic Paganism and Druidry

The terms Celtic Paganism and Druidry are often used interchangeably. Both beliefs originated from similar European countries, like Ireland and Scotland, and shared many similarities. However, they aren't the same, and their differences give each belief its own identity and characteristics.

This chapter explains Druidry and Celtic Paganism, highlights their differences, and discusses Celtic myths, deities, rituals, and festivals.

Celtic Paganism vs. Druidry

The Celts were a group of tribes from central Europe who shared the same language, culture, traditions, and religious beliefs. Interestingly, modern scholars referred to them as "Celts," but no one knows what they were originally called. It is believed each tribe had its own name rather than having an umbrella term like the Greek or Roman empires.

They practiced Celtic Paganism, an ancient polytheistic religion that worshiped more than one deity and spiritual practices and beliefs. They believed their gods existed in everything around them, so they highly revered nature.

Druidry, called Druidism, was a shamanic religion that originated in Britain, particularly Wales. It involved communicating and working with the spirits and belief in the power of holistic medicine in causing and treating diseases. The religion was part of the Celtic culture hence its association with Celtic Paganism. It was a religious belief and a magical practice.

The Druids considered oak trees sacred.
https://unsplash.com/photos/KnBHXJzqIRs?utm_source=unsplash&utm_medium=referral&utm_content=creditShareLink

The druids were Celtic priests and leaders of the Celtic religion and Druidry. The word "*druid*" is derived from the Celtic word "*doire*," meaning oak tree or wisdom. The druids considered the oak tree the most sacred of all trees.

They were extremely wise and knowledgeable and acted as judges, philosophers, scholars, and doctors, connecting people to their deities. They played a huge role in Celtic society; kings and peasants often sought their wisdom. Unfortunately, the druids passed down their teachings orally and prohibited their followers and students from using the written word. As a result, most information scholars have about Celtic Paganism and druids is second-hand knowledge.

Julius Caesar invaded Britain in 55 BC. He witnessed the druids and their influence firsthand. In his book, "The Gallic Wars," he mentioned that they were key figures in the Celtic faith, performed religious duties, interpreted all aspects of the religion, and were highly respected among the people who often turned to them to settle disputes. They even used their influence to prevent wars. He added that when a person committed a crime, the druids had the power to pass judgment.

Caesar also mentioned in his book how the druids urged their members to memorize all their teachings and religious beliefs instead of writing them down because they didn't want their knowledge to spread among the commoners.

The druids were so powerful and untouchable that the Celtic laws and rules didn't apply to them. For instance, they didn't serve in the army or pay taxes. They were different from the Celtic pagans, the same way a regular person differs from a priest. They influenced the people with their knowledge and power, and the Celtic pagans sought their help with all matters.

Both religions believed in the afterlife, worshiping multiple deities, and highly revered nature, so people often confuse the two. Celtic Paganism is a broad term describing all pagans in the Celtic society, including the druids. However, *Druidry* refers to a group of people within the Celts. In other words, all druids were Celtic pagans but not all Celtic pagans were druids. Druidry focused more on nature and magic than mythology and cosmology, which were significant in Celtic Paganism.

Nowadays, Druidry is a spiritual path and a way of life, but some people still treat it as a religion. It became a diverse belief welcoming people from all religions, including Celtic pagans. However, not all are polytheists. They can also be monotheists (worshiping one god), duotheistic (worshiping two gods), pantheists (believing god is the universe), or animists (believing everything has a spirit, including inanimate objects). However, one thing they all have in common is that nature is sacred, a belief they share with their ancient ancestors.

Neo-Celtic pagans or Celtic Reconstructionism is based on ancient Celtic beliefs and incorporating its practices into modern society. Similar to their ancestors, they are polytheistic and revere nature. It is separate from neo-Druidry as each religion has its own identity.

The Celtic Belief System and Spirituality

The Celtic pagans highly revered nature, especially trees they considered sacred, and worshiped their deities in natural settings like cliffs, bushes, rivers, and lakes. They held the Moon, stars, and Sun in high regard and believed them supernatural. They considered animals like horses, bulls, stags, and boars sacred and often engraved them on armor and weapons for protection.

The Celtic pagans worshiped over 400 gods and goddesses and appeased their deities by offering them their favorite food, drinks, weapons, and valuable objects. Unlike ancient Roman and Greek deities, they didn't have human characteristics. In other words, they didn't have weaknesses, nor were they influenced by worldly desires. The Celts believed the deities controlled the universe and mankind and hugely influenced people's daily lives.

Since the Celts revered nature, they associated their gods and goddesses with natural settings and phenomena like lightning and the Sun. Many of their deities were depicted as a trio representing three divinity aspects. For instance, the goddess Matronae was a triple goddess associated with fertility, power, and strength.

Although they had a deity for everything like the Moon, Sun, hospitality, and chance, the main focus was on the gods and goddesses associated with the main concerns of people, like protection, healing, warfare, hunting, and tribal identity.

They believed in supernatural beings like elves and fairies who existed in nature and were very powerful creatures. They could help and bless mankind, but if mistreated, they would reveal their ugly side and cause harm and disease.

The Celts believed in the afterlife, which is clear from their burial rituals. They buried the royals and the rich with all their belongings, such as food, utensils, pottery, jewelry, clothes, board games, armor, weapons, and everything else needed for their journey to the underworld. Their leaders and prominent individuals in the state were buried in wood-lined chambers and dressed in their best attire.

Although not much is known about their afterlife, scholars believe the Celts regarded the otherworld as the same as this life but without its negative aspects like grief, pain, loss, and diseases. As a result, they didn't fear death and welcomed its arrival. Cremation was common in ancient Paganism, which they borrowed from Mediterranean cultures.

Myths and Cosmology

Understanding the cosmology of the Celtic religion, its deities, and sacred symbols can only be done through myths and legends. Like many ancient cultures, the Celts had a rich and fascinating mythology, and people still tell their stories in Ireland, Wales, and various parts of Europe.

King Arthur's Journey to Annwn (The Spoils of Annwn)

This legend is based on the poem "Preiddeu Annwn." Preiddeu means spoils, and Annwn means the underworld. King Arthur took his men and three ships and traveled to the underworld to take a cauldron that belonged to the lord of Annwn. The cauldron had magical powers. It would only boil the food of the brave, not the coward.

Arthur arrived at Caer Sidi, the fort of the otherworld or the fairy fortress. He found the cauldron in a cave over a fire with nine maidens breathing over it to keep it burning.

The poem is very mysterious and dark. One line echoed in multiple stanzas, "Except seven, none returned," indicated that only Arthur and six of his men survived this disastrous journey. However, he returned victoriously with the cauldron.

Interestingly, the poem doesn't only reflect Arthur's bravery and his ability to survive the journey to the underworld, but it also highlights the cauldron's significance in Celtic mythology. One of the most famous cauldrons belonged to Cerridwen, a mythical Celtic witch and the goddess of inspiration. She used it to make magical potions that bestowed wisdom and knowledge on whoever drank them. The cauldron could resurrect the dead.

Cerridwen's cauldron appeared in another legend with Bran the Blessed, the giant King of Wales. He gave it as a wedding gift to his sister Branwen and her husband Math, the King of Ireland. However, when war broke out between Wales and Ireland, Bran decided to take back the cauldron. The story shared many similarities with the legend of King Arthur. Bran also took the journey with some of his bravest knights, but only seven survived. He died in battle and went to the underworld like King Arthur in the Quest of the Holy Grail, who went to Avalon after his death. Some scholars believe Cerridwen's cauldron is the Holy Grail that King Arthur searched for all his life.

The Legend of the Tuatha Dé Danann

The Tuatha Dé Danann were the tribes of gods in Celtic cosmology. Before they arrived in Ireland, a group of giants called the Firbolgs ruled the land. The Firbolgs were surprised by the arrival of the Tuatha Dé Danann and weren't prepared for battle, making it easy for the gods to vanquish them and rule Ireland. Their King Nuada, the god of hunting, was badly hurt during the battle and lost his arm. It made him unfit to rule because, according to the Tuatha Dé Danann laws, the king should be in perfect health and shape.

Although the other gods loved and respected him, Nuada had no choice but to step down from the throne. He appointed Breas to take his place but only for seven years until Nuada found a way to restore his arm. Breas's mother was from the Tuatha Dé Danann, but his father belonged to the Fomorians, a group of monstrous giants. Breas was a vicious and unfair king who favored the Fomorians over the Tuatha Dé Danann during his rule.

Creidhne, the god of metalworkers, succeeded in creating a silver hand for Nuada. The king returned to his kingdom and took back his throne. Although Breas knew his position was temporary, he was angry when he had to give up the throne. However, the people rejoiced since they loathed him and loved Nuada. Breas went to Balor, the leader of the Fomorians, to sow the seeds of war between the two tribes. Balor agreed to fight the gods. Some of the Firbolgs joined them since they wanted to get back at the Tuatha Dé Danann for taking their kingdom. Although he had one eye, Balor was a very strong and cruel giant. He fought hard in the battle, killing many of the Tuatha Dé Danann, including their King Nuada.

Lugh, the god of justice, nobility, and the Sun, was a powerful and honorable deity and the grandson of Balor. Although he was half Fomorian from his mother's side, he was nothing like Breas. Nuada trusted him and chose him to lead the army. Lugh proved to be a great leader. He used his magic to strengthen the army and provided them with weapons.

When Lugh found out on the battlefield that his grandfather killed Nuada, he was adamant about avenging his king. He killed Balor, leading to the Tuatha Dé Danann's victory.

Lugh became a hero and was chosen to rule the Tuatha Dé Danann. He was a just, brave, and wise king. He used his kinship with the Fomorians to establish peace between the two races.

The Main Gods and Goddesses in Celtic Paganism

Lugh

Lugh was the god of judgment, oaths, and nobility and one of Celtic Paganism's most popular and strongest deities. He had many titles, but the most famous was Lámfada, meaning "of the long arm." It referred to the magical and powerful spear he often used on the battlefield. He was a king, judge, and poet known for his many skills. The god was responsible for distributing talents among mankind. Caesar mentioned him in his books as one of the most prominent gods in Celtic Paganism and highly revered among the people.

Interestingly, Lugh was a trickster deity who would steal, cheat, and lie to defeat his opponents.

When Lugh wanted to join the court of Nuada, he traveled a long road to reach Tara, the hall of the kings. When he asked to enter, the guard told him he must have a unique skill to be allowed in the court. Lugh showed him his many skills as a poet, blacksmith, wheelwright, and many others. However, the guard told him they already had someone with that particular talent each time. Lugh used his wit and told the guard they didn't have a champion with all these skills. The guard realized Lugh was right and let him in the court. It was in the court where he proved himself and impressed Nuada to the extent that he became the leader of his army.

The Morrigan

The Morrigan (or *Morrighan*) was the goddess of fate, battles, wars, and death. She supported Celtic heroes and gods, helped the Tuatha Dé Danann in battle, and prophesied their victory against the Fomorians. She could transform into a beautiful woman to lure men or into a raven and fly over the battlefields. It is believed if she appeared to a warrior in the water while he washed his armor, he would die that day in battle. She had the power to decide who lived and died during a war.

According to some legends, she was a triple goddess. Nemain, Macha, and Badb were three goddesses called the Morrigan. However, in other legends, they were her sisters.

One of the most famous myths associated with the Morrigan is her story with Cu Chulainn, a mighty warrior, and Lugh's son. Cu Chulainn was at war with Queen Maeve, protecting the Irish city of Ulster from the queen's army. The Morrigan, who was always present on battlefields, fell in love with the young warrior when she first saw him. She transformed into a beautiful woman to seduce him right before the battle, but he rejected her advances.

The Morrigan was furious and vowed vengeance against the man who broke her heart. She transformed into an eel, swam to Cu Chulainn, and attacked him. However, the strong warrior punched the eel, not knowing it was the goddess, and hurt it badly. She recovered fast, transformed into a wolf, and drove a herd of cattle to Cu Chulainn. He hit the fox in the eye with a slingshot, blinding the Morrigan.

The determined goddess transformed again into a cow and drove a herd of cows to stampede the young warrior. He survived the attack and broke the Morrigan's leg. Cu Chulainn finally went to battle and won.

On his way home, he saw an elderly woman milking a cow. She had one broken leg and was blinded in one eye. He conversed with her, and she offered him a glass of milk. After drinking the milk, he blessed the woman, which cured her of all the injuries. The woman was the Morrigan, who tricked Cu Chulainn into healing her.

On his way to another battle, he saw a woman washing bloody armor, which was a bad omen. However, he didn't let the image deter him and continued his journey to the battle.

Unfortunately, the brave hero was mortally wounded, but he managed to tie himself upright to a large stone to scare his enemies. While taking his last breath, a crow landed on his shoulder. Was it the Morrigan? No one knows.

The Dagda

The Dagda was the Tuatha dé Danann chief and the father deity of Ireland. He was the god of Druidry, magic, fertility, agriculture, seasons, knowledge, life, and death. Druids highly revered him since he bestowed on them wisdom and knowledge of magic. He was the most powerful and skilled of all the Celtic deities, and his name meant the good god.

He was often depicted carrying a club in one hand that could end and resurrect someone's life and a magic cauldron over his shoulder containing an endless supply of food. He also carried a harp which he used to change the seasons.

The Dagda was the husband of the Morrigan and the brother of Nuada. He was mortally wounded during the battle against the Fomorians at the hands of Balor's wife, Cethlenn.

Brigid

Brigid (also spelled *Brighid*) was the Dagda's daughter and the goddess of life, fertility, motherhood, passion, fire, water, serenity, and spring. She was associated with poetry and healing. Like the Morrigan, she was a triple goddess, with two other goddesses also called Brigid.

Her name meant "the exalted one." She is often compared with the Catholic saint Brigid since they both have more in common than just their names. Ancient and modern Celt pagans celebrate the goddess during the Imbolc festival in February. She hugely influenced people by inspiring poets and writers and protecting newborns and mothers.

During the battle between the Tuatha dé Danann and the Fomorians, Brigid lost her father and her son Ruadán. When she heard the news, she ran to the battlefield and saw her son's lifeless body. Her heart was broken, and she wailed in a loud lament that became known as keening. It was the first time someone expressed their grief in that manner, and everyone in Ireland felt her pain. It is how keening became a tradition among Irish women mourning their dead.

Cernunnos

Cernunnos was referred to as the horned god, the deity of wild places and beasts, and the protector of the forests. He ruled over nature and animals and was associated with vegetation and fertility. He was a mysterious god, and only a few things were known about him.

As a result of his association with animals and forests, Cernunnos led an uncivilized life. The animals were his servants, and he was often depicted as surrounded by snakes, wolves, and elks. He could tame animals and bring predators and prey together.

The Celtic Festivals

The Celtic calendar is called the Wheel of the Year. All Celtic festivals focused on seasonal changes since they impacted agriculture and harvest.

Samhain (October 31)

Samhain celebrated the end of summer and the harvest season. The veil between the realm of the living and the dead is weak during this time, allowing ancestors' spirits to travel to this world. People would often place an extra plate on the dinner table to remember and honor their departed loved ones. Halloween and its traditions were all borrowed from Samhain.

Yule (Winter Solstice December 20-23)

Yule takes place on the shortest day of the year and is a time of rebirth and renewal. People light candles and bonfires to celebrate the Sun's return during this festival. It is similar to Christmas and includes decorations like trees and mistletoe.

Imbolc (February 2)

This festival takes place between winter and spring and celebrates the goddess Brigid. It also celebrates the end of the winter and the arrival of spring. People would light candles and place them in every room to represent the Sun's return.

Ostara (Spring Equinox March 20-23)

Ostara represents new beginnings and celebrates the arrival of spring and the end of darkness. It is similar to Easter and shares the same traditions, like decorating eggs.

Bealtaine (May 1)

Bealtaine celebrates spring, warm weather, and all nature's gifts. During this festival, people light bonfires for protection against evil forces and celebrate by dancing. Many couples get married on this day because it is associated with passion and lust.

Summer Solstice (June 20-23)

This festival takes place on the longest day of the year during the warm weather when nature is strongest. People celebrate outdoors, throw feasts, eat delicious food, and light bonfires. The fairies are usually active during this time, so people leave them offerings.

Lughnasadh (August 1)

This festival is associated with the god Lugh who threw a feast and held competitions to honor his foster mother, Tailtiu, the goddess of labor and childbirth. She was responsible for clearing the fields so mankind could harvest their plants. However, it was a hard process, and she died. Therefore, Lugh honored her with this festival. People celebrated it by lighting bonfires.

Mabon (Autumn Equinox September 20-23)

Mabon takes place when the day is equal to the night. During these days, the Sun weakens in preparation for winter. People express their gratitude for the harvest and all nature's blessings.

A Simple Ritual to Do at Home

Create a spring altar at home during Bealtaine to celebrate the festival. You can use the altar for worship and prayers all year long.

Instructions:
1. Choose a room or a small space in your home away from distractions.
2. Clean it from dust and cleanse the area with burning sage (burn a bundle of sage and let the smoke purify the area).
3. Place a white cloth over the altar.
4. Add candles, fresh flowers, statues, symbols, or pictures of your favorite Celtic deity and nature symbols. Keep it simple.
5. Write your intentions for the rest of the year on a piece of paper and leave it on the altar.
6. Light a candle every day to energize the altar and reaffirm your intentions.
7. Don't ignore your altar and keep it maintained.

Disclaimer: Burning sage and candles are fire hazards, so caution is advised.

Celtic Paganism is a rich and fascinating religion. Each god has a different personality, power, and domain, adding to the religion's magic and allurement. Many things can be learned from Druidry and Celtic Paganism, like respecting nature and animals and believing that mankind isn't superior but one with all the gods' creations.

Chapter 3: Asatru: Norse Paganism

Asatru Paganism is a fascinating and mysterious practice that has existed since before the Viking era. It is the modern interpretation of ancient Norse belief systems, blending spiritual practices with mythology, rituals, and ethical beliefs. This chapter delves into the specifics of Asatru Paganism, exploring its origins and cosmology, discussing its spirituality and beliefs, naming the gods and goddesses they pray to, and introducing readers to their rituals. Whether or not you subscribe to the spiritual teachings of Asatru Paganism, it is an intriguing way to trace the roots back through history, uncovering past traditions.

What Is Asatru?

Asatru is a modern revival of the ancient pre-Christian belief system of the Icelandic people, commonly known as Norse Paganism. This spiritual tradition dates back to the first century CE and was practiced by many Germanic tribes living in Northern Europe. The religion was almost completely forgotten until its revival in the late 19th century.

The origins of Asatru can be traced to Old Norse literature, particularly the Eddas, which are collections of ancient stories and poetry chronicling religious beliefs and historical events from Scandinavian cultures. These texts describe the gods and goddesses worshiped by these tribes and their cosmology and rituals. In particular, they talk about Odin and his brothers, Vili and Ve, creating the world from nothingness on Yggdrasil (the World Tree). They provide insight into how various magical runes were used for divination, healing practices, and other traditional customs, such as feasting on holidays like Yule (the winter solstice) or celebrating Freyr's Day around the summer solstice period.

The origins of Asatru can be traced to the Eddas.
https://commons.wikimedia.org/wiki/File:Edda.jpg

In addition to this literary evidence, archaeological excavations discovered artifacts suggesting that these belief systems were incredibly widespread during this period, from Sweden down to what are now Germany, Austria, Hungary, and parts of Romania. For example, bronze figurines depicting Odin were found throughout Scandinavia dating back to 600 CE, while grave goods, like swords, were discovered in graves, depicting Viking-era burial practices.

The revival of Asatru began in Iceland in 1972 with Sveinbjörn Beinteinsson leading an initiative known as "The Ásatrúarfélagið" (or "Ásatrú Fellowship"). This organization sought to restore traditional beliefs and practices under a new name, Ásatrú, meaning "faith in the gods." Since then, various organizations have been established around Europe, including Norway's Foreningen for Nordisk Religions (FNR), Denmark's Forn Siðr/Nordisk Hedendom, Britain's Odinic Rite/The Odinic Rite Association (ORA), and Germany's Ring der Götter und Geister (RiGG). Despite its relatively recent revival, compared to other belief systems like Christianity or Islam, Asatru has quickly become one of the largest religions, with millions of adherents worldwide practicing their faith according to its core tenets.

Cosmology

The cosmology of Asatru is a subject that its adherents have fiercely debated. The religion heavily focuses on the Norse Pantheon and its various myths and stories. At its heart, Asatru centers on the concept of honor, not only for yourself but also for all living things. This honor is expressed primarily through reverence for the gods and goddesses in the Norse Pantheon and adherence to a heroic code of conduct known as "the Nine Noble Virtues."

At its core, Asatru recognizes nine realms:
- The three worlds beneath Earth, Niflheim, Muspellsheim, and Svartalfheim
- Midgard (the world)
- Jotunheim (a realm occupied by giants)
- Asgard (home of the gods)
- Vanaheim (the realm of the Vanir gods)
- Alfheim (the realm of the light elves)
- Helheim (the underworld)

Within these realms live numerous beings, such as dwarves, elves, giants, gods, and goddesses. Each realm is inhabited by its spiritual entities, including deities and other supernatural figures with specific areas of influence relevant to human life.

The relationship between humans and these divine entities determines their fates in this life and their afterlife. In Asatru belief systems, humans are part of an interconnected web of existence where every action affects them somehow. Therefore, it is important to maintain a balance within this web to achieve spiritual and physical harmony.

Asatru has two components: faith in Odin and other Norse deities and a warrior ethic requiring followers to meet challenges head-on with courage and strength. This warrior ethos greatly emphasizes courage, sacrifice, personal honor, strength in battle, and loyalty to friends or clan members.

Beliefs and Spirituality

Ásatrú, and the closely related Norse Paganism, is a polytheistic faith venerating many gods and goddesses. It is rooted in pre-Christian practices in Viking Age Scandinavia but has been influenced by modern interpretations of Norse mythos from sources like the Poetic Edda and Prose Edda. Asatru. Norse Paganism is based on the belief that deities are living beings with whom followers can interact directly, often through rituals or offerings. The gods are seen as protectors or guardians of humanity, and their worship helps ensure success and prosperity. In addition to the Pantheon of gods, adherents venerate land spirits (*landvaettir*), ancestors (*disir*), and various other spirits.

Asatru - Norse Paganism is a faith that celebrates nature's power in all forms and seeks to maintain a balance between humanity and the gods. The religion aims to live harmoniously with the gods and nature. Practitioners believe everything around them is alive and sacred, from rocks to trees, rivers, oceans, fire, animals, and birds. Everything has an elemental spirit that can be honored if respected.

At its heart, Asatru is an animistic religion. Adherents see everything around them, from animals and plants to mountains and rivers, as having their own spirits, energies, or powers. Animism is reflected in many customs, such as offering libations to land spirits when entering new territories or asking permission from tree spirits before cutting down trees.

Asatru practitioners believe fate is predetermined by a person's actions in past lives (*wyrd*) or how others affect you (*orþrótt*). Therefore, every action has good and bad consequences, so people should strive for righteousness to ensure good fortune for now and in future lifetimes. This belief ties into one of the core values held by Asatru, honor your word (*hlautbúa*). Being honorable means being truthful with yourself and others which helps build trust between people while maintaining respect for yourself by keeping your promises.

The gods and goddesses of Asatru are integral components of this belief system. They represent various facets of nature and humanity, such as fertility, war, justice, family life, death, love, and wisdom. These deities are viewed as powerful supernatural beings and role models whose stories provide insight into how humans should conduct themselves. Worshiping these gods brings blessings if done properly. However, neglecting them can bring misfortune or tragedy to yourself and those around you.

The gods are considered distinct entities with their wills and personalities. They are viewed as spiritual forces rather than abstract concepts or metaphors. In addition, rituals are associated with honoring the gods, such as blot sacrifices where animals were partially or wholly sacrificed as food offerings during celebrations like Yule or Winternights (*Hallowtide*). These ceremonies were thought necessary for maintaining relationships between humans and their deities, allowing them access to Valhalla after death. Upon their deaths in battle or from natural causes, they would be welcomed into Odin's hall. Other rituals pertain specifically to holidays like Ostara, where eggs were exchanged between family members signifying renewal, and Thor was honored by lit bonfires on Midsummer night. These rituals were meant to honor the gods and as a reminder that living harmoniously among each other is possible if faithfully adhering to values with those sharing the same beliefs.

By honoring the gods through ritual, adherents seek to live according to the moral code of Asatru - Norse Paganism: The Nine Noble Virtues. The Nine Noble Virtues of Norse Paganism, known as Asatru, are moral codes guiding and shaping the conduct of practitioners. These virtues come from an ancient pagan religion and are still practiced today.

1. **Courage:** To be courageous in all situations, take risks, accept challenges with strength, and be resilient in times of difficulty.
2. **Truth:** To live honestly and openly, never lie or deceive others, and strive for truth.
3. **Honor:** To maintain a noble character at all times, uphold the highest standards of behavior with integrity, and strive for excellence in everything.
4. **Fidelity:** To remain true to your word, relationships, and commitments – and stand by loyal friends and family.
5. **Discipline:** To practice self-control, stay focused on achieving goals, and practice moderation.
6. **Hospitality:** To provide generous hospitality when hosting guests and treat them as honored family members.
7. **Industriousness:** To work hard to gain knowledge, develop skills, earn money, build material wealth, and always improve self.
8. **Self-Reliance:** To rely on self rather than depending on others, take responsibility for your actions, and not rely on luck or fate.
9. **Perseverance:** To remain strong despite adversity and never give up, even when faced with great hardship or opposition.

Another important aspect of Asatru spirituality is saga telling, stories about mythological characters from Norse lore, usually around a campfire after dinner at private gatherings or ritual events. Through listening to these tales, participants learn more about their culture's history while discovering spiritual lessons within their narratives about heroism, courage, loyalty, self-sacrifice, honor, justice, truthfulness, compassion, humility, and wisdom. Furthermore, these tales offer insight into how adherents should live according to a worldview based on Nordic traditions. It helps adherents become better versed in integral aspects of Heathenry's values, ethics, morals, and laws.

Significantly, Asatru - Norse Paganism is an ever-evolving faith tradition. Today's beliefs and practices span from humanism to Reconstructionism, from viewing the gods as metaphorical constructs to approaching them as distinct beings. The diversity of belief within the community allows followers to explore their spiritual paths while honoring their cultural heritage and connecting with other pagans globally. Regardless of how you view or practice Asatru - Norse Paganism, its fundamental core is an appreciation for life and nature and a commitment to working toward a balance in the physical and spiritual worlds. With this understanding, adherents can strive toward living a meaningful life filled with joy, wisdom, and fulfillment.

Gods and Goddesses

Asatru, or Norse Paganism, is based on the belief in multiple gods and goddesses who inhabit different realms and guide humanity. Many gods and goddesses are associated with Asatru, but some are more important than others. These major deities include Odin, Thor, Freya, Freyja, Frigg, Loki, Heimdall, and Idunn. These major gods and goddesses are closely linked to Asatru beliefs and are essential to Norse Paganism. They guide, protect and offer wisdom to their people while being respected as powerful deities. By understanding these deities more, practitioners can better appreciate aspects of the faith, such as its mythology and symbolism.

1. Odin

Odin is considered the chief god of Asatru. He is known as a powerful deity who rules over Asgard, the realm of the Aesir gods. He is a wise teacher who gives advice and wisdom to humankind through prophetic revelations. Odin is associated with war and magic. It is said that he sacrificed his eye to gain wisdom. Odin had magical powers allowing him to shape-shift into animals or people. He carried two magical artifacts, an eight-legged horse named Sleipnir, which could travel between worlds without getting tired, and an all-seeing eye called Odin's Eye, which allowed him to see into many places simultaneously.

2. Thor

Thor is Odin's son and the primary god of thunder in Asatru mythology. Thor is the god of thunder and lightning and rules over storms. He is one of the most famous figures in Norse mythology. Known for his strength and courage, he could wield a magical hammer called Mjölnir, which controlled lightning bolts. Thor protects Asgard from giants who attack it, using his magical hammer to strike them down. He is a guardian of humankind, protecting them from harm and helping them through difficult times.

3. Freya

Freya is a goddess of love, beauty, fertility, and war in the Asatru Pantheon. She has many associations with nature, such as fertility, love, and sexuality. Freya is a strong protector of her people, particularly those most vulnerable. She often takes the form of a beautiful falcon when in battle, leading warriors to victory.

4. Freyja

Freyja is Freya's twin sister and is associated with similar aspects like fertility and love. She wears a necklace of precious stones called Brisingamen, which grants her great powers. Freyja's power lies in her ability to see into the future and guide mankind. Freyja has the power to cause strife among enemies if someone wrongs her or her loved ones. She can take on different shapes at will and travels around Midgard (the realm of humans) on her chariot pulled by cats.

5. Frigg

Frigg is Odin's wife and goddess of marriage and motherhood in Asatru mythology. Like Freya and Freyja, she is associated with love and fertility. She is a wise and loving mother figure who looks after all Asgard's inhabitants.

6. Freyr

Freyr is one of the Vanir gods associated with peace, fertility, and prosperity in Norse mythology associated with peace. Freyr was known for his great wealth but was generous, giving away his possessions freely even when it led him into trouble or danger. He gave away his last valuable possession, his magical sword, to win over Gerd (a giantess), whom he wanted to marry. He was renowned for having an enormous appetite. It became a running joke among other gods and goddesses that he was never satisfied – no matter how much food they served him.

7. Tyr

Tyr was another god associated with war, specifically for courage and bravery on battlefields. Tyr offered warriors strength and courage when their natural reserves were depleted. Tyr was admired by many for his selfless actions like bravery. He sacrificed one hand, so the Fenrir wolf would not break free from its bonds, preventing *Ragnarok* (the twilight age and the end of the world) from happening prematurely.

8. Loki

Loki isn't technically considered a deity but an immortal trickster who caused much mischief throughout the Norse Pantheon. He is depicted as sometimes playing pranks and other times causing destruction and malice purposely. However, Loki's primary function is to nurture humankind, ultimately assisting birth and the new beginning after Ragnarök.

9. Heimdall

Heimdall is the Aesir race's herald protector. He is in charge of guarding the Bifrost Bridge connecting the Asgard realm to mortals' Midgard. His sharp, keen senses allow him to detect even the slightest disturbance miles away, making perfect sense of why he is appointed sentry of the gateway between realms.

10. Idunn

Idunn is the goddess of youth and immortality in Asatru mythology. Her magical apples are said to keep the gods young and prevent them from aging or dying. Idunn is associated with fertility. It was believed that eating her apples could lead to increased fertility in women.

Festivals and Celebrations

Asatru and Norse Paganism are ancient religions steeped in tradition dating back centuries. As part of these ancient traditions, various festivals and celebrations are associated with the religion honoring gods and goddesses and important events throughout the year. These festivities vary from region to region and provide an opportunity to reconnect with the old ways and celebrate spirituality within the community.

The Viking Age calendar was divided into two distinct seasons, summer (light) half and winter (dark) half. In modern times, March 20th marks the beginning of summer, and October 31st marks its end. Each season is symbolically linked to certain deities honored through celebration at each season's change. Summer is associated with the Norse gods Freyr and Freyja, while winter is associated with Odin and Ullr.

One of the most important Asatru festivals is called Ostara, which takes place at the spring equinox (March 20th). This ancient festival celebrates the rebirth of nature after a long winter and symbolizes renewal. It was traditionally celebrated by offering gifts to the gods, feasting, and singing songs in their honor. The festival is closely associated with Easter as both share similar themes, such as fertility and new beginnings.

The summer solstice (June 21st) or Midsummer's Day marks another important event on the calendar for Norse Paganism followers. This celebration honors Freyja, who presides over fertility and the beginning of summer. It is believed that on this day, the Sun god, Baldur, rises from the dead to bring light and life back into the world. People celebrate Midsummer's Day by gathering for bonfires, feasting, and dancing.

Lammas (August 1st) marks the harvest season and celebrates Freyr, who presides over wealth and abundance. This festival is a time to give thanks for all that was harvested during the year and for people to share in its bounty. Lammas is known as Loaf Mass because it was traditionally celebrated by offering bread made from grain from the harvest to Freyr.

The winter solstice (December 21st) is another important festival marking the year's longest night. This day is associated with Odin, who presides over death, wisdom, magic, and runes. People celebrate this day by giving offerings to Odin and lighting candles in his honor. The Yule log is traditionally burned, bringing warmth and light into homes during the long winter months.

Walpurgis Night (April 30th) celebrates Ullr, the god of hunting, skiing, and archery, and his divine wife, Freya. This celebration is not in traditional Viking calendars but has become one of the most popular festivals among modern-day Norse Paganism followers. It was originally celebrated by lighting bonfires in honor of Ullr and Freya and making offerings to them. Today, it is celebrated more as an opportunity for people to get together for feasting and merrymaking.

The festivals associated with Asatru and Norse Paganism allow people to connect with their ancient spiritual roots while celebrating the seasons' changes. They are a time for honoring gods and goddesses, giving thanks, sharing food, and enjoying fellowship within the community. These festivities help keep these ancient traditions alive in modern times and ensure that the old ways will never be forgotten.

Rituals

Blot

The Blot ritual is one of the most important rituals in Asatru. It consists of offering sacrifices to the gods or goddesses and hallowing them with ale, mead, and other libations. The ritual's purpose is for practitioners to honor the gods and goddesses and ask for their blessings in return. It is a way to thank the gods and goddesses for all they have done and given to the practitioner.

You need an altar, a chalice or other vessel for libation, an offering like food or drink (usually mead or ale), runes, incense, candles, and something to represent each god or goddess honored to perform this ritual. If a group is performing the ritual, it's best to each bring something representing each god or goddess being honored so they can all be acknowledged during the ceremony.

Instructions:
1. Set up your altar with items, such as offerings and representations of each god and goddess being honored.
2. Light candles and incense before saying a short prayer invoking all of the gods and goddesses being honored.
3. Pass around your chalice filled with mead or ale so that everyone can take part in hallowing it.
4. Once everyone has taken part in hallowing your offerings, take turns speaking words of gratitude for whatever each god and goddess has done for you
5. Pour your libation on the ground near your altar, representing their acceptance of your offerings.
6. When finished speaking words of thanksgiving and pouring out your libations, close your invocation with another short prayer thanking them again
7. Close down your ritual space.

Sumbel

Sumbel is a ritual with roots in the ancient Asatru religion. It is practiced today by modern adherents and as a regular part of a ceremony or at special events. The word Sumbel comes from the Old English term "drinking together." It is an important part of many gatherings and celebrations in Asatru.

The Sumbel ritual aims to honor the gods, ancestors, and other spirits and celebrate life's milestones. During the ritual, participants pledge or make oaths to each other and share words of encouragement. It strengthens bonds between family members and friends while demonstrating respect for each other's beliefs. Additionally, participants are encouraged to reflect on their actions and how they impact those around them.

The structure of the ritual is similar to a toast-making ceremony. However, the content varies depending on the event being celebrated or honored. Generally, Sumbel rituals involve drinking mead (or juice if mead isn't available) from a horn or cup known as "the blessed cup," passed from one person to another clockwise. Each time someone takes a sip from the cup, they honor someone else in attendance with kind words or symbolism, like pouring some drink out onto the grass or the earth outside to honor land spirits. Once everyone has had their turn with the blessed cup, there is usually laughter and joyous celebration accompanied by singing and folk dancing.

Seiðr

Seiðr is an Old Norse magical ritual widely practiced in pre-Christian Scandinavia. It is believed to have been used for various purposes, such as healing, divination, protection, and even cursing. It was most commonly performed by shamans or chieftains believed to be in touch with the gods and could influence events through their magic. The ritual usually involved chanting or singing, drumming on a hide, ecstatic dancing, and trances. The shaman would call upon otherworldly powers, such as elves and dwarves, to help them accomplish their tasks.

To perform a Seiðr ritual in the Asatru tradition creating the right environment for a successful magical event is necessary.

Instructions:
1. You need a sacred place where you can perform the ritual without any disturbances from outside sources. It can be inside or outside your home.
2. Prepare yourself mentally and spiritually for the ritual, like meditating beforehand, so that your mind is clear and open for what will happen during the ritual.
3. Once these steps have been taken, it is time to set up the space for the ritual. The space should face northwards toward Asgard (the realm of the gods).
4. A fire should be burning. At least two fires with candles placed around them.

5. Light some incense. It must be lit before chanting (usually with herbs like Juniper).
6. The chanting should consist of mantras associated with certain gods or spirits. Each god and spirit has its particular sound and will summon its energy into your circle.
7. Chanting can usually last up to ten minutes or more, depending on the depth of your trance.
8. When the chanting is completed, create a shield with runes. These runes should be chosen according to what you want to achieve with your Seiðr ritual, whether answers from the gods about something specific or casting a spell on someone.
9. End your ritual by thanking all of those who participated.
10. Close your sacred space until the next time.

Knowing how and why to do a seiðr ritual is important. It is an offering or prayer to gods and spirits so that they will intervene on your behalf when guidance or assistance is required. This makes the seiðr ritual exceptionally special and powerful in Asatru tradition.

Chapter 4: Germanic Paganism

"Germanic" refers to a tribal collective of Indo-Europeans from the Iron Age who spoke the Germanic languages and settled in Germany, the British Isles, and Scandinavia. This chapter focuses on Germanic pagan cultures like the Icelanders, the Anglo-Saxons, the Danes, and more. Besides providing information regarding their pagan traditions, the chapter offers a historical overview of Germanic pagan tribes and their migrations.

The History of Germanic Pagans

While it's unclear when the Germanic tribes arrived in Northernmost Europe, by 750 BCE, they were commonly established in the territories of modern-day Denmark and southern Scandinavia. Their popularity expanded so much that 500 years later, they migrated toward central Europe. Their migrations caused conflict with the Celts, who were also expanding their cultural influence. However, the Celts were defeated by the Germanic tribes. Later, the population growth caused several tribes to invade each other's territory, while others migrated to Italy, Spain, and Gaul. In the 5th century AD, many tribes merged, forming tribes like Anglo-Saxons, the Danes, the Swedes, and others.

Germanic tribes had rituals similar to the Celts, such as sacrifice.
https://commons.wikimedia.org/wiki/File:Olaus_Magnus_-_On_the_Geats%27_Worship_and_Sacrifice.jpg

These migrations, conflicts, and coexisting beliefs of the different Germanic tribes left their mark on their belief systems. Archaeological findings indicate that during the Roman Iron Age (before 400 AD), the Germanic tribes practiced similar spiritual rituals as the Celts. They had similarities in how they offered sacrifices to deities and conducted divination, and, like the Celts, they believed in forming a spiritual connection with nature. However, they had a unique tradition of burning their dead before burying them in the ground. Some traditions were still practiced in the Germanic Iron Age (from the beginning of the 5th century), but soon after, Germanic tribes were converted to Christianity. However, this was an earlier and less festivity-based form of Christianity, so many Germanic Pagan practices survived through oral traditions or written records. Records from the early middle ages show a widespread reverence toward the Old Norse deities, priests, and natural phenomena.

The Icelanders

The Icelanders were a small group of Germanic pagan people who arrived on the shores of Iceland at the end of the 9th century. They had and maintained very similar beliefs to their Germanic pagan ancestors. They venerated the same gods and worshiped ancestors and nature with the same fervor. Their belief system is one of the most preserved from the North Germanic pagan tribes. They were preserved by oral tradition and recorded in sagas and, even more famously, the Poetic Edda, one of the most widely known sources of Norse mythology.

The Anglo-Saxons

According to historical records, the Anglo-Saxons arrived on the shores of Great Britain at the end of the 5th century. They carried pagan beliefs very similar to Norse Paganism. However, their religion later diversified under the influence of separation from the rest of the pagan tribes and later the pressure from other religions. They worshiped Woden (Odin), the highest god of their Pantheon. According to Anglo-Saxon beliefs, Woden was the god of death, who guided the departed souls toward their path in the afterlife. Unlike other more grounded authority figures they worshiped, he was universally feared, like the gods Tiw (Thir) and Thu (Thor).

Besides the indications of natural-based worship places, Archeological findings suggest the Anglo-Saxons might have built pagan temples. There, they held rituals addressing their deities and offered sacrifices to them.

The Danes

The Danes were a Germanic tribe that arrived in southern Scandinavia around the middle of the 6th century. They spoke Proto-Norse, and later Old Norse, and had similar beliefs to the North Germanic tribes. Their religion is woven with elements of Norse Paganism, worshiping Thor, Odin, and Frey. Like many other Germanic pagan tribes, the Danes left behind other deities. However, they participated in ancestral worship and maintained many original customs even after converting to Christianity in the 10th century. For example, they used the same burial practices and practiced runic divination. Besides the traditional Germanic Christianity that appeared in the 10th century, the Danes were influenced by Arian beliefs (a much older version of Christian doctrine emanating from 3rd-century Egypt).

Key Points in the Germanic Pagan Belief System

Germanic Paganism is an umbrella term for several closely related pagan beliefs interlocked in one large system. Most of these beliefs and traditions stem from the Old Norse religion, but in the medieval period, these were heavily influenced by Christian theology. Like their ancestors, the Germanic pagan belief system is also polytheistic. Many religious practices of the Germanic tribes of North-Western Europe were lost.

However, it is known that even before medieval times, Germanic Paganism was more about individual worship and family traditions than about the tribes having one organized religion. Still, their traditions had a consistent framework. They typically revolved around the deities and the cycle of life. It is believed that the ancient Germanic tribes had traditions around their belief in the underworld, continued life after death, a world of ancestors in the heavens, and reincarnation. Germanic mythology has several variations of the creation myth. According to the most famous one, there was nothing but a magic void in the beginning. Odin and his brothers created the Earth from it and later gave life to humankind from two lifeless tree trunks.

Most Important Gods and Goddesses

According to ancient Germanic pagan mythology, the Pantheon of gods comprises two tribes, Vanir and Aesir. It is believed that once these tribes realized neither side could win, they made peace.

The Aesir

Odin

Odin was the ruler of Aesir and the god of kings and Germanic noblemen. The common people, however, rarely turned to Odin for help, and he wasn't widely worshiped. In Germanic Paganism, Odin is known as the god of poetry. There are many stories about how Odin brought the sacred mead of poetry to the gods. According to one of these stories, the mead was created from the blood of a wise god, Kvasir, who was killed by dwarfs. Odin stole it and escaped with it in the shape of an eagle, carrying the mead in his crop.

Odin was also known for his propensity to incite fights among the warriors and turn them against each other to recruit heroes in Valhalla. The dead heroes would join him in the final battle against Ragnarök. Odin was also said to create powerful magic that could make dead men talk. He was a magician, a shapeshifter, and a powerful shaman, who could enter a trance and journey into other worlds. When he visited the dead, he was always accompanied by two ravens and two wolves. The birds were his messengers, informing him of happenings in the otherworld and the world of mortals.

In Germanic Paganism, Odin is portrayed as the god of the hanged. This belief stems from the Old Norse myth of Odin suspending himself on the Yggdrasill (the tree of life) to gain wisdom.

While Odin was often considered untrustworthy by the commoners, he was a sovereign deity. The descendants of the ancient Germanic tribes across England and Scandinavia regarded him as their uppermost divine ruler. Foundations of dynasties are still attributed to Odin, and for centuries, he was offered extraordinary sacrifices for his blessings. While he was typically presented with animal sacrifice, human sacrifice was not uncommon. However, the latter stems from Roman writers who magnified the gruesomeness of Germanic pagan practices to instill fear and misconceptions.

Thor

Thor was a widely worshiped deity. He was one of the last deities people turned to before the end of the pagan period in Germanic lands. Thor is Odin's son. His name is derived from the Germanic word for thunder. Myths describe Thor as the champion of the gods, raving about his victories over giants. His success is often attributed to his hammer, Mjölnir. He had adventures with other mythical creatures, like the cosmic serpent Jörmungand. This creature lived in the ocean surrounding the world. After pulling the monster out of the vast waters, Thor fails to kill it and is expected to face it again at Ragnarök.

Unlike his father, Thor is the god of the common Germanic pagan people. Places across England and eastern Scandinavia were named after him. He was worshiped as the god of thunder and was thought to bring rain and ensure a good harvest. Warriors were guided into battles by him and called on him to assist in their military enterprises.

Thursday (Donnerstag in German) is named after Thor, meaning Thor's day. Modern Germanic pagan practitioners still believe Thor travels in his chariot in the sky toward the east daily, and thunder is the sound of his chariot.

Balder

In Germanic mythology, Balder is another son of Odin. Unlike Thor, Balder is a much more patient god. He had prophetic powers and even foretold his own death. According to the lore, his mother made all creatures take an oath not to harm him. However, after the mistletoe refused to take the oath, Loki, the trickster god, tore it off, handing it to the blind god, Höd, who inadvertently used it to kill Balder. When the gods sent to retrieve Balder's soul from Hel, he couldn't be released because the goddess of death was not paid what she asked in return.

According to her decree, everyone should have grieved Balder's death. Loki disguised himself as a giantess and refused to mourn Balder, so Balder had to remain dead.

According to the Danes, Balder wasn't an innocent deity whose death was supposed to be a mournful event. They believed him to be a vicious demigod. Balder and Höd were constantly fighting for the hand of Balder's wife, and Höd killed him in one of their many fights. Across later Germanic pagan beliefs, Balder was often described as a dying spring god. However, given that these depictions gave him Christ-like features, they might have been influenced by Christian beliefs.

Loki

Although Germanic pagans count Loki among the Aesir, he is considered an outsider to this tribe. His father was a giant, and probably his mother, too. Loki is the father of Jörmungand, the serpent surrounding the world. He fathered Hel, the goddess of death, and Fenrir, the wolf whose destiny is to be chained until Ragnarök. According to their beliefs, Loki is bound but will undoubtedly break his chains when Ragnarök comes. He will honor his father and his progeny by joining the giants in the battle against the gods.

While Loki was known to deceive the gods, he also helped them at times, particularly Odin and Thor. He is a trickster deity who can change shape at will. For example, in one tale, he was depicted fighting Heimdall in the form of a seal for a necklace. Another poem describes his adventure in Freyja's residence in the form of a fly. Across Germanic pagan beliefs, Loki represents a source of impulsive intelligence. Under his influence, a person can act with unpredictable maliciousness.

Minor Aesir

Minor deities in the ranks of the Aesir included Heimdall, Rigr, and Tyr. Forever at odds with Loki, Heimdall and the trickster god are bound the kill each other at Ragnarök. According to the lore, Heimdall was born from nine mothers, who were presumed sisters and probably giantesses. Heimdall lived at the edge of the Aesir world, guarding it against the giants. He has incredibly powerful hearing and can pick up on anything in either world.

Rigr can possibly be one of the faces of Heimdall but is also said to be the father of humankind. Rigr bore children with three females, who gave birth to the three different races according to German pagan beliefs.

Tyr was a prominent divine figure during the early days of Germanic Paganism but has almost been forgotten. He only had one hand because the wolf Fenrir removed the other. He is a brave god and is believed to be the son of Odin. Some sources claim that rather than being a deity, Tyr was fathered by a giant.

Frigg

Like her husband, Odin, Frigg is depicted in several ways in various Germanic sources. Some show her as the weeping and self-sacrificing mother of her children, including Balder. Others described her as a libertine who wasn't afraid to live passionately. The latter sources claim that her misconduct was responsible for the poor fame and the brief banishment of Odin from the divine Pantheon.

The Vanir

The Vanir were another group of Germanic pagan deities. Most were associated with health, fertility, and weight. Unlike the Aesir, the Vanir rarely participated in battles nor influenced the outcome of conflicts and wars as the Aesir did.

Freyr

The eastern Danes notably celebrated Freyr, the son of Njörd. They believed that Freyr regularly departed eastward, traveling on a giant wave with his chariot following him. According to the Germanic tribes inhabiting the modern-day territory of Sweden, Freyr traveled inside the chariot. He brought blessings of fertility and a good harvest to the barren lands that lay beforehand in this Northern European territory. According to an Icelandic saga, when people began to cultivate crops, Freyr appeared to watch over the field. Therefore, the fields became sacred.

One of the most epic adventures of Freyr was the conquest of Gerd, a giant maiden who later became his wife. There are several renditions of this myth. One claims that Gerd was taken to the otherworld, and to get to her, Freyr had to overcome the rules of life and death. According to another version, the maiden was held captive by winter, bringing frost giants, whom Feyr had to battle for her. The latter story became a nature-based fertility myth in which Freyr is the Sun god who frees Gedr, the ruler of the Earth. Once the Earth is freed in Spring by Freyr, nature becomes fertile after winter.

Several animals were sacred to Freyr, including the horse and the boar (known for its high fertility). The Danes had a similar deity called Frody, who was responsible for the land's prosperity. Since he was also carried in a chariot, some said he was Freyr under a different name. Freyr was believed to be the ancestor of the Yngling, the Swedish royal family.

Freyja

Freyja is Freyr's sister (and wife for a brief period) and the goddess of love, fertility, and beauty, indicating very similar responsibilities to her brother. According to the lore, she is often surrounded by fine items, including jewelry. One of her most famous pieces was the Brísingamen necklace, forged by dwarfs and later stolen by Loki. Loki and Heimdall famously fought over it. Freyja was said to be a faithful wife, often depicted weeping tears of gold when her husband was away. However, some sources claim that she was rather promiscuous. The latter probably stems from the tales of her practicing magic unknown to many - even between the gods. This was seiðr magic, which Odin used on a few selected deities. Similarly to Odin, she guided the souls of those who fell in battle.

The fertility goddess Freyja is associated with animals. It represents a controversial feature of a fertility goddess associated with the otherworld, which wasn't present outside Germanic pagan beliefs.

Due to Freya's dual nature, she is often symbolized by a wide range of items, including a dog and a snake (alluding to their connection to the otherworld) or fruit, the ultimate symbol of fertility. Some tribes had a similar goddess under different names, like the goddess Nehawho, worshiped by Germanic tribes in central Europe.

Festivals and Celebrations

In traditional pagan fashion, the Germanic tribes didn't like to confine their worship and ritual practices within walls. Across the Germanic pagan world, nature-based practices were widespread, with the most common places of worship being sacred groves and woodlands. Tribes in Scandinavia, England, and continental Europe held their rituals and ceremonies near trees and wells. When they built temples and similar closed worship sites, they did it near sacred trees and wells.

According to Roman sources, the early Germanic pagan tribes did not visualize their deities in human forms. Whatever items were used to represent the divinities, they were effigies denoting divine power rather than any form. Later, these symbols became anthropomorphic in nature.

Most common Germanic pagan practices were (mostly animal) sacrifices offered to gods and goddesses. During these sacrifices, the number nine was significant. They presented nine heads or other organs to the gods to appease them and placed the offering near or in a sacred grove where they left it for nine days. They believed anything they put near the grove became sacred.

They conducted sacrifices by sending items where no one could access them, like the bottom of a lake. Or, they would simply burn the sacrificial object for similar purposes. They held sacrificial festivals (one of the rare festivals celebrated in ancient Germania), which involved festive meals and libations. During these celebrations, large public offerings were made, often gathering one or more tribes, where sometimes wooden figures were sacrificed instead of people.

Another Germanic pagan tradition was the offering of weapons to the deities. Archeological findings suggest the tribes would often throw into a lake or sacrifice weapons rendered useless after a battle. Interestingly, weapons were always sacrificed separately from other sacrificial items. Besides their own useless weapons, the tribes often offered their defeated enemy's weapons to the gods. Most offerings were made to Odin as an expression of gratitude for his blessings that led the winning party to victory. The sacrifice affirmed the connection between Odin and his worshipers and ensured this short-tempered god always stayed on their side.

Burial ceremonies were widespread. They often burned and buried the departed and their possessions, including animals and enslaved people. Before their burial, the animals and enslaved people were treated with the same respect as their masters, often receiving the same food, drink, and other privileges. During the intensive migration periods, the burial ceremonies were held on the shore or on ships.

While unified festivals were rare among the Germanic pagans, those that existed revolved around the deities. They held a public celebration of the gods and goddesses on the days associated with them. The modern names of the days of the week originate from the deities the Germanic pagans associated with them. Publicly honoring the deities on their sacred days gave the people a sense of community and reaffirmed their connection to the divine. Some festivals and celebrations were in reverence to the seasons. Early on, the Germanic pagans celebrated seasons equivalent to winter, spring, and summer. However, later groups, like the Icelanders, held only winter and summer celebrations.

Blot Ritual

The blot ritual was common in different Germanic tribes and is practiced today. Traditionally the blot is offered to a deity on the days associated with them. You can make a blot to a different deity each day of the week. Here is an example of an offering to Thor:

Ingredients:
- A glass or bottle of a natural drink. You can use water, natural juices, or anything that doesn't contain artificial flavors.

Instructions:
1. Find a quiet space in nature before sundown. If you're doing the ritual on a Thursday, you'll start by facing east as Thor travels toward the east.
2. Hold the cup or bottle between the palms of your hands and move it toward your belly. Aim to hold it at the level of your belly button.
3. Visualize how your energy travels from your palms and belly toward the bottle or cup and the drink inside it.
4. Take a deep breath through your nose and slowly exhale, chanting the name of Thor (or another deity).
5. Now that the liquid has been charged with your essence, it's ready to be offered to the chosen deity.
6. Pour some of the liquid out, and raise it toward the sky, offering it to the deity.
7. Hold the cup or bottle with both hands, place it in front of your belly, and repeat the chanting nine times.
8. Now the liquid has been charged with the power of the deity you're holding the blot for.
9. Raise the drink once again toward the sky, acknowledge the deity's blessings, and drink from it.
10. Don't drink it all at once, but take small sips throughout the evening. This way, you'll feel the deity's power coursing through you, slowly enveloping you with protection and healing.

Finding Connection to Nature

Nature plays a pivotal role in Germanic pagan traditions. Finding your connection to nature's energies is a ritual of empowerment and a way to establish balance in your life. Spending time in nature or near an element of nature in the morning is a great reminder to take as you continue your day.

Instructions:
1. After waking up in the morning, pick up a charm, talisman, or representation of the deity or spirit you've felt connected to recently and carry it with you.
2. Make your coffee, tea, or breakfast, and find a piece of nature. If you can go outside in a garden or terrace, do it. If you can't go outside, open a window and sit beside it. Alternatively, you can sit beside a potted plant; this also represents nature.
3. Whichever option works for you, have your drink or breakfast doing it.
4. While you do, use nature's power to ground yourself and calm your mind.
5. When relaxed, take the charm, talisman, or whatever object you've picked up beforehand and meditate. You don't have to have a particular notion. Wanting a connection to nature and your spirituality is more than enough.
6. You can meditate for as long as you want, but 5 minutes is usually enough. The entire exercise (along with consuming your drink or meal) doesn't have to last longer than 15 minutes.
7. You will feel empowered and ready to take on the day's challenges.

Chapter 5: Slavic Paganism

This chapter introduces Slavic Paganism, referring to the beliefs and practices of the ancient Slavic people of Eastern Europe. While Slavs are usually subdivided into East, West, and South Slavs, the core beliefs and deities are much the same across all Slavic territories. Besides learning about the most prominent Slavic gods and goddesses, myths, and festivals, you will learn to master a beginner-friendly Slavic pagan ritual at the end of the chapter.

The Slavic Pagan Path and Its History

In a typical pagan fashion, Slavic beliefs and traditions were passed down orally, and the ancient religion was also heavily influenced by Christianity. Very few records of the old Slavic belief system exist. One of the few written sources that exist is the "Slavic Primary Chronicle," originating from the early 12th century. It compiles the religious beliefs of the Slavs, mainly those revolving around the two most prominent Slavic gods, Perun and Veles. According to this source, a peace treaty in the 10th century between the Eastern Slavs and the Byzantine Emperors resulted from the Slavs' desire to maintain the balance between the powers of the two deities.

Dazhbog, the Sun god.
Mhapon, CC BY-SA 4.0 <https://creativecommons.org/licenses/by-sa/4.0>, via Wikimedia Commons: https://commons.wikimedia.org/wiki/File:Dadzbog.jpg

Some records indicate that in the 10th century, Eastern Slavs worshiped a distinct Pantheon of gods known as the Pantheon of Prince Vladimir. It included the deities Dazhbog, Hors, Stribog, Simargl, and Mokosh. Some are still celebrated today, but the traditions revolving around others have been lost.

While records about West Slavic pagans are more prolific than those depicting the Eastern Slavs' beliefs, these stem from the 12th century, when most Slavs converted to Christianity. Unfortunately, their customs were recorded by German priests who didn't speak Slavic languages. Consequently, many of the meanings behind the traditions were lost in translations. "Chronica Slavorum," a document created in the late 12th century, mentions Czrnobog, Zorya, and Perun, some of the most important gods to the Western Slavs. It also mentions several unnamed Slavic deities with multiple heads.

Statues of Slavic deities were discovered in many Slavic regions. These were tall stone monuments erected in higher places. Many statues have multiple faces, indicating that different deities had several aspects. Some sites contained several shrines dedicated to various aspects of the same deity. Other findings included a human-sized wooden statue with two heads, hinting that some cultures might have viewed the deities as people with supernatural abilities. Russian mythology experts agree that many archeological remains of the different ancient Slavic cultures and religions have common roots.

Key Points in the Slavic Pagan Belief System

Slavic mythology points to a polytheistic belief system. However, it emphasizes the worship of deities with several aspects. Many Slavic gods have several faces and personalities and could exhibit different powers. They're celebrated at altars or shrines, near or in nature. Slavic Paganism is a religion relying heavily on nature. Its followers aim to respect nature as much as possible, emphasizing the importance of using natural resources correctly.

Slavic pagan practitioners often use nature's power in rituals, spells, and ceremonies, representing it with air, earth, fire, and water. They also employ salt, which has cleansing properties and is often used to purify the self, the home, objects, or magical tools. They burn salt to get black salt, which has even more powerful cleansing properties because it is burned with healing flowers. Flowers, herbs, and spices represent another way Slavic pagans use nature's power in their practices.

For Slavic pagans, the Sun and the Moon are the most potent sources of protective and healing energies. Basking in the sunlight can provide the empowerment to face upcoming hurdles. Whereas gazing into the moonlight will cleanse a person's energy. Similarly, leaving objects under the Sun or Moon will charge them with their respective powers.

The Slavic pagans have several popular divination methods. One of the most widespread involves melting wax and pouring it into water. As the wax hardens in the water, it forms certain shapes, which are analyzed to determine what messages they can reveal about future outcomes.

The Most Important Gods and Goddesses

While it's unclear whether the Slavic pagans ever had a unified Pantheon of gods, they do have several deities that were and still are worshiped across several Slavic regions.

Perun

Perun, the god of thunder, watched over the sky and sent lighting. He was a god of war and had many similarities with the Norse gods Odin and Thor. Perun was associated with oak trees and active parts of nature and is often described as a heavily masculine entity.

According to a famous Slavic myth, in ancient times, a sacred oak tree was the home of all living creatures in this world. The tree's top branches symbolized heaven; its trunk and lower branches were reserved for the earth, while its roots represented the underworld. Perun resided on the top branches to see everything that happened in the world. In ancient times, Perun was typically honored in nature, and later devotees built temples and shrines for him. These were erected in higher places so the messages could reach Perun more easily.

Dzbog

Dzbog was the god of fortune and the governor of fire and rain. According to Slavic legends, he gave life to the crops in the fields at the beginning of time and every spring since. His name can be translated into abundance or "the giving god," implying that he can provide plentiful bounty and harvest. Dzbog was the patron of the hearth fire, another element allowing a home to be filled with something everyone needs: love and spiritual prosperity. Devotees made offerings to Dzbog by a burning fire, asking him to ensure they would always have fire to warm up during the colder months.

Veles

Veles was the infamous shapeshifter god. Unlike Perun, who only brought rain and lighting, Veles brought storms that did more damage than good. Due to the rivalry between these two deities, Veles was often said to use tricks to get close to Perun. For example, one tale describes him taking on the form of a serpent and slithering up the sacred oak tree to see what Perun was doing on the top branches. According to other legends, Veles stole Perun's bride and children and hid them in the underworld. In many aspects, Veles is very similar to Loki, the Norse Pagan trickster god. He is said to practice magic and sorcery to bring hurdles and mishaps into people's and gods' lives.

Belobog and Czernobog

Belobog and Czernobog represent the rules of opposite forces. The first was the god of light, while the other was the god of darkness. Some say they were not two deities but the two aspects of the same deity. The latter belief stems from the lack of evidence about Belobog or Czernobog being worshiped individually. While the origins of either deity are unknown, most Slavic Pagans agree that Czernobog (the black god) was a deity with dark propensities. He was probably cursed early in his life and became associated with death and misfortune. If people weren't careful enough to protect themselves, Czernobog could easily cause plenty of calamity in their life. In some legends, he is described as a demon, indicating the source of all things evil. On the other hand, Belobog was the total opposite. His name is translated as the white god and was often prayed to for blessings, guidance, and protection from evil, including Czernobog.

Lada

Lada was the goddess of love and beauty, associated with spring and fertility. She was the Slavic patron of matrimony and newlyweds. Lada was often summoned to weddings to bless the newlywed couples union. She had a twin brother Lado, who had similar associations and was also called upon to bless mortal unions. Other sources claim that Lada and Lado were two faces of the same entity, unified in the perfect balance of feminine and masculine energy. It allowed them to bring harmony to couples' lives. In some sources, Lada is given a motherly role. She is said to be nurturing toward those who follow and celebrate her. Lada is similar to the Norse goddess Freyja, who is also associated with love, beauty, and fertility.

Marzanna

Marzanna was the Slavic goddess of winter and death. She was responsible for the death of the earth during the winter months. However, she is believed to be dead with the soil, only to be revived again in the spring. Some tales claim she is reborn as Lada, while other myths affirm that Lada only takes over the rule over the earth in the spring. In several Slavic traditions, Marzanna is symbolized by an effigy, either burned or drowned during a ritual signifying the end of a life cycle and the beginning of the new one.

Mokosh

Mokosh was the fertility goddess and the protector of women. As a motherly figure, she watched over pregnant women and their children's birth and ensured their well-being as they raised their children. She is linked to domestic duties associated with women, including cooking, weaving, and spinning. Among the Eastern Slavs, Mokosh was often seen as a source of fertility. They made offerings to her and represented her with breast-shaped stones in rituals and ceremonies, presenting these at her altar. Other times, she is depicted with male reproductive organs because, as a fertility deity, she is also responsible for male fertility.

Svarog

Svarog was the fire deity, the god of the Sun, similar to Hephaestus in Greek mythology. He was associated with metalsmithing and metal forging. In Slavic mythology, Svarog was the creator of the world. Svarog sometimes worked alongside Perun, and the two deities are often blended into an all-mighty father god. According to the lore, Svarog created the world of mankind in his sleep. His dreams shaped the Earth and the world as everyone knows it. Some sources claim that Svarog continues to shape the world as he continues to sleep, and when he wakes up, the world will end.

Zorya

In Slavic mythology, Zorya is the goddess of dusk and dawn. She is associated with the Morning and Evening Star, indicating that she has at least two aspects. Her morning aspect (Zorya Utrennjaja) opens the gates of heaven at dawn. Her evening aspect (Zorya Vechernjaja) closes the same gates at dusk. According to a well-known legend, Zorya dies at midnight following the Sun's death. She is reborn again in the morning, just as the Sun is revived at dawn.

Festivals and Celebrations

The world of the Slavic pagans is cyclical, meaning all events repeat each year. They usually follow the changes in nature and the seasons. The major events were celebrated over a series of colorful festivities incorporating different rituals, offerings, and feasts.

By observing Slavic mythology, it's easy to understand the most notable dates of their calendar. The Slavic calendar is based on the lunar year. This year begins on the first day of March, similar to the traditional calendars of other ancient pagan cultures. Several well-known holidays in modern-age calendars are based on Slavic pagan customs. Halloween and Easter are two examples of how the widespread traditions of worshiping Slavic deities have turned into modern holidays.

Another example is the festivities held in the name of Veles. He was the god of the underworld and was celebrated among Slavic pagans on the last day of the year. Below are the most prominent Slavic holidays.

Koleda

Koleda is the celebration of the beginning of the Slavic pagan year. In ancient times, this was a New Year celebration that took place during the winter solstice in December. After Slavic Paganism fell under Christianity's influence, Koleda was unified with the Christmas holidays. However, the name of the festivity has remained Koleda among those who follow the Slavic pagan path and is often celebrated through ancestral customs. According to different Slavic myths, the holiday is either named after Kolyada, the god of winter, or Koliada, the goddess who revives the Sun every morning.

Koleda is a deeply spiritual festival. Many devotees use it to celebrate with rituals, spells, and ceremonies as spiritual cleansers. This tradition is tied to the role of spirits in the Salvic belief system. The primary purpose of Koleda celebrations is to ward off evil spirits and toxic energies from around the home and self and replace them with good spirits and positive vibes.

In ancient times, Slavic people dressed up as animals and dedicated prayers and songs to the good spirits, often inviting them through dance. Sometimes, people let aggression take over them and would get into fights. It was a ritual allowing one last opportunity for the bad spirits to control the body, after which they had to leave people's lives. Dressing up as animals was a way to honor Veles, the god of the underworld, animals, and forests. Simultaneously, Koleda is also dedicated to another deity, Perun, the god of thunder. The two gods represent two sides of the same coin. One brings destruction, while the other creates. They establish natural abundance, which must be honored.

Koleda is a time of bonding for the Slavic pagan communities. Food is often shared in the community during this time. Depending on the local customs, people gather to eat, talk, and light a fire. The children are charged with gathering wood and bringing food to community gatherings. While they are doing this, they sing Kolyadki songs, which speak about wishes for happiness, prosperity, and peace for everyone at the end of the year.

Komoeditsa

Komoeditsa is a spring holiday dedicated to the bear god. The celebration occurs in early March, at the spring equinox, when people offer food to this deity by leaving it in the forest. In ancient times, people presented the bear god with crepes with homemade jelly or jam to sweeten up this deity. While this food offering ritual is rarely practiced in modern times, its new version, Maslenitsa, is very popular. Due to Christian influences, Maslenitsa has been blended into the Western Christian Carnival and is celebrated around the same time. It's a week-long festival ending with a ceremony called Forgiveness Sunday. During this ceremony, family, friends, and community members gather to share a feast and ask each other for forgiveness. They might exchange presents, often giving small items the other likes to show their remorse for whatever wrong they've done to them during the year.

In some territories, Komoeditsa is dedicated to the goddess Lada and her bother Lado, the Slavic deities who gain most of their powers around the spring equinox. Their strength lies in their ability to blend male and female energies, symbolizing the fertility of nature and new life. Consequently, the holiday celebrates the revival of nature in spring.

Krasnaya Gorka

Another springtime festivity in Slavic pagan cultures is Krasnaya Gorka. This festival allows young people to meet, share a conversation, get to know each other, possibly fall in love, and find their future spouses. While the festival lasts for several days, at the culmination, young maidens and men dress up, meet, dance together, and sing songs about love and happiness. In some regions, it is said that if a young single person stays at home during Krasnaya Gorka, they will remain single for the rest of their lives.

In other regions, the young folks are encouraged to paint eggs in yellow or green and share them. Besides bringing people together, this ritual honors the ancestors. Traditionally, young people make cakes and crepes. However, before that, they would exchange eggs and oil, which helped them remember and share their ancestors' wisdom.

Kupala

Kupala, known as Kupala night or summer solstice, is a summer holiday, traditionally celebrated in mid-June, on the shortest night of the calendar year. During these festivities, people gathered to sing cheerful songs, prank each other, and tell jokes. According to Slavic traditions, women were the most fertile on Kupala night, and many couples used it to conceive healthy children. Traditionally, it was believed that the night or the day before and after Kupala night increased the chances of a healthy birth.

Besides singing and dancing, people used water to symbolize their wishes for fertility and cleaning. Women who wanted to conceive would bathe in magically charged water to boost their feminine energy. Young maidens would decorate their hair with fresh flowers during the day, and when the night came, they took off their adornments and threw them into the river. The flowers thrown into the water represented a desire for a romantic relationship and marriage. If the flowers floated on the water's surface, the girl's wishes for marriage were granted. However, if the flowers sunk, no relationship or wedding would follow. Boys would enter the water, attempting to rescue the flowers and spark the interest of the maiden whose flowers they caught. In some regions, Kupala worship involves walking to the forest at twilight to find a fern flower, which was said to have magical properties and blooms only on this night. In other places, Kupala is simply celebrated by community members gathering beside a large log fire, singing, dancing, and jumping through the fire.

The Festival of Perun

The Festival of Perun is celebrated at the end of the summer. For the Slavic pagans, it is a way of greeting the new season and mourning the previous one. It's said that around this time of the year, powers in nature shift from feminine to masculine.

People celebrate the festival of Perun by offering and sacrificing to this deity. They know he was the power to keep nature favorable during autumn, so it's crucial to keep him appeased. The festivities often include lighting a sacred bonfire and wearing protective amulets, which were charged with positive energy beforehand. In ancient times, men would later wear these amulets when in battle. During the festival, warriors would show off their warfare skills. At the end of the festivities, men reenacted a fight between Perun and Veles, with the former being the victor.

The Festival of Mokosh

This festival marks the autumn equinox in Slavonic religions. It represents the beginning of the harvesting season and is celebrated with the Harvest festival (known as Rodogosch or Tausen). The festival culminates with a ritual dedicated to Mokosh, the goddess of the Earth.

Mokosh has often represented wet Earth, indicating her feminine energy. Devotees would light a fire in the hearth or, in modern times, a candle to honor the goddess. This goddess can be represented by a spinning wheel during rituals and ceremonies performed in her honor during the festival.

At the festival, women often ask Mokosh to help protect their families and keep them together and nurtured with positive energy. The celebration of Mokosh has decreased in popularity as the Slavic culture became more patriarchal. Nevertheless, there are still regions where she is celebrated through the old customs.

A Ritual to Connect with Nature

Since Slavic Paganism is a nature-based religion, the followers often perform rituals to enhance their connection to nature. The following easy-to-do rite can be conducted whenever you want to bring yourself closer to nature to obtain its blessings, including fertility and revival. It's recommended to perform this ritual on a sunny day in a place with plenty of sunlight, as the Sun is crucial in nature's fertility.

Ingredients:

- The representation of the four elements of nature, air, fire, earth, and water (you can use a candle for the fire)
- The representation of a fifth element, salt
- A representation of a natural being, for example, a plant or a small animal
- A representation of a deity (if you are working with one)
- Natural incense (like tree sap)
- Sunlight, or, alternatively, the representation of the Sun

Instructions:

1. Find a quiet space for your ritual, preferably near a window on a sunny day. If you have an altar, perform it there. Alternatively, go to a natural clearing and perform the ritual directly under the Sun. This way, you only need to carry a few ingredients to the ritual place (as some will already be there).
2. Gather your supplies and place them in front of you. The four elements should be placed at the four corners of the space in front of you, while the fifth should be set in the middle.
3. Light the candle and place the plant or animal in front of you.
4. Take a deep breath and focus on your intention. Feel free to do it now if you call on a deity to empower your connection with nature.
5. When you're ready, address nature with the following words:

    "Sacred nature, I respect and worship you.

    You center and ground me, and I wish to remain close to you.

    Please bless me with plentiful, and I will forever be thankful for your gifts."
6. Look up towards the Sun, and feel how it helps you re-form your connection to nature. Feel how you are revitalized and ready to take on life's challenges.
7. Later, you might even get inspired to be more productive or fertile in different areas of life.

Chapter 6: Greek Polytheism

Greek polytheism, often referred to as Hellenism, encompasses a wide range of beliefs and practices. At its heart, Hellenic polytheism comprises multiple spiritual paths arising from Greece's vibrant and complex ancient mythology. This polytheistic religion honors a diverse Pantheon of gods and goddesses, each with unique personalities, stories, and powers. Practitioners seeking to revive the ancient Greek religious practices into a modern pagan religion are known as Hellenes, Hellenic Reconstructionists, or Hellenic pagans. Conversely, other practitioners claim to have inherited the original ancient traditions passed down through the ages. Regardless of your path, Greek polytheism is a journey of discovery and a chance to explore the rich cultural heritage spanning thousands of years.

Greek gods and goddesses.
Immortality113, CC BY-SA 4.0 <https://creativecommons.org/licenses/by-sa/4.0>, via Wikimedia Commons. https://commons.wikimedia.org/wiki/File:Mt-olympus_gods.jpg

Many people compare the Hellenistic belief system with Paganism. While the word *"pagan"* has historically been used to describe any non-Abrahamic religion, Hellenism is very much an umbrella term. The comparison of Hellenism with Paganism depends on how a person defines "Paganism." For instance, if you consider Paganism to be referring to non-Abrahamic faith, then yes, Hellenism does fall under the umbrella of pagan religions. However, if you define Paganism as the modern-day goddess-worshiping, Earth-based religion, Greek polytheism would not fit this description. Hellenic polytheism is more focused on the ancient Greek gods and goddesses.

Moreover, some Hellenes take issue with being labeled as pagans since many people assume all pagans are Wiccans, which is not the case for Hellenes. Some scholars argue that the term "pagan" was never even used by the Greeks themselves to describe their religions. This theory suggests that the origins of the word "pagan" comes from a Latin word, translated to "rustic" or "of the countryside," and was originally used by early Christians to refer to non-Christians. Outside society's mainstream, it was never used in Greece. More so because worship in ancient Greece was decentralized, and each city had its own cult and traditions. Therefore, the Greeks didn't consider themselves a unified entity like the Romans.

So, while Greek polytheism shares many similarities with Paganism, particularly its modern revival, people should be aware of the distinctions between these two belief systems. Hellenism is a rich and complex religion encompassing many aspects of Greek philosophy, religion, and social life. It emerged in ancient Greece during the classical period and profoundly influenced the development of Western civilization. This chapter comprehensively explains the Hellenistic belief system, including its historical development, customs, and practices. From its origins to modern-day celebrations, you will discover all aspects of Greek polytheism.

How History Shaped the Greek Belief System

Ancient Greece is known as the cradle of Western civilization, but how did this come about? How did the polytheistic belief system come into existence? What were the factors that shaped Hellenism and Greek mythology? The roots of the Greek belief system can be traced back to prehistoric times when the locals believed in numerous spirits and deities associated with nature. With time, cultural influences, and historical events, this belief system further developed into the complex Pantheon of gods we know today.

One of the most important factors was the influence of neighboring cultures. The Greeks were exposed to many religions and mythologies from other civilizations, including Egypt, Mesopotamia, and the Near East. They adopted and adapted many of these stories and beliefs, incorporating them into their religion. Each civilization contributed its unique elements to the development of Greek mythology and religion:

1. Egyptian Influence

The Greeks were fascinated by Egyptian religion and mythology, which had a complex Pantheon of gods and goddesses associated with specific natural phenomena and animals. The Greeks were particularly interested in the god Thoth, associated with knowledge and writing. Over time, they identified Thoth with their god Hermes, who became known as the messenger of the gods and the patron of travelers and merchants. It led to the development of Hermeticism, a spiritual tradition that combined elements of Greek and Egyptian religion and philosophy.

2. Mesopotamian Influence

The Babylonian creation myth of the god Marduk slaying the primordial dragon Tiamat and creating the world from her body was particularly influential on the Greek creation myth. In Greek mythology, Zeus and his siblings overthrow their father, the Titan Cronus, and establish themselves as the rulers of the universe. The Mesopotamian myth also influenced the story of the Greek hero Perseus, who slays the monster Medusa and uses her head as a weapon.

3. Near Eastern Influence

The Near East was also a major cultural influence on the Greeks, with the ancient city of Ugarit being a major center of trade and culture in the eastern Mediterranean. The Ugaritic Pantheon of gods and goddesses, including Baal, the god of storms and fertility, and Anat, the goddess of war and hunting, particularly influenced the Greeks. Many of the stories and attributes of these gods and goddesses were adapted and incorporated into the Greek Pantheon. For example, the goddess Athena, who was associated with war and wisdom, could have been influenced by the Near Eastern goddess Anath.

The polytheistic belief system of ancient Greece was influenced by neighboring cultures and shaped by the writings and works of Greek poets, playwrights, and philosophers. Here are some ways these individuals contributed to the development of Greek polytheism:

4. Hesiod and Homer

Hesiod and Homer were two of the earliest and most influential Greek poets. They wrote epic poems featuring gods and goddesses as major characters. Hesiod's "Theogony" and Homer's "Iliad" and "Odyssey" provided the Greeks with a foundation for their understanding of the gods and their relationships with each other and with mortals. Hesiod's "Theogony," in particular, details the world's creation and the gods' genealogy, an established hierarchy of deities, and helped define their roles and characteristics.

5. Greek Tragedy

Greek tragedy, which emerged in the 5th century BCE, was a major cultural force contributing to the development of Greek polytheism. Tragedy often featured stories about the gods and their relationships with mortals. It explored themes of fate, divine justice, and the limitations of human understanding. Playwrights such as Aeschylus, Sophocles, and Euripides used their plays to explore complex questions about the nature of the gods and their relationship with humanity. For example, in Sophocles' "Antigone," the heroine defies the city's laws to honor the divine law, leading to a conflict between the state's authority and the god's authority.

6. Greek Philosophy

Greek philosophy emerged in the 6th century BCE and contributed to the development of Greek polytheism. Philosophers like Plato and Aristotle used their works to explore the nature of the gods and their relationship with the world. For example, Plato's concept of the *Forms* suggested that the gods represented reality's highest and most perfect form. On the other hand, Aristotle argued that the gods were the unmoved movers of the universe, responsible for setting the world in motion but not actively intervening in human affairs.

The Greeks also believed in the concept of fate, which was closely tied to their understanding of the gods. They believed the gods controlled the events of the world and humans were subject to their whims. This idea was reinforced by the oracles revered throughout Greece as sources of divine wisdom and guidance.

Greek Polytheism and Spirituality

As you know by now, Hellenism is based on the worship of a Pantheon of gods and goddesses. At the core of Hellenic belief is the idea that everything in the world is interconnected. It is expressed through the concept of cosmos – referring to the order and harmony of the universe. The gods are believed to play an important role in maintaining this order, and their worship is a way of maintaining the balance between the natural world and human society.

The gods are a central part of Hellenic belief and practice. Each god or goddess is associated with a specific aspect of the natural world, like the sky, the sea, or the Earth. They are associated with virtues such as wisdom, courage, or beauty. Hellenic practitioners often develop personal relationships with the gods through prayer, meditation, and offerings. The gods are not seen as omniscient or omnipotent but are believed to have their own personalities, desires, and areas of influence.

Myths and legends are an essential part of the Hellenic tradition, woven into the very fabric of Hellenic culture. They are not just stories but repositories of wisdom, knowledge, and insight into the universe's workings. Through these myths and legends, Hellenic practitioners connect with the gods, understand the natural world's mysteries, and gain a deeper appreciation of their place in the cosmos.

Storytelling is vital to Hellenic practice, with many rituals and ceremonies incorporating myths and legends. These stories are often ritualized, with the storyteller acting as a conduit between the gods and the listeners. Through the power of storytelling, Hellenic practitioners can connect with the divine, gain insight into their lives, and strengthen the bonds with their community. One myth that shaped the belief system of Hellenism was Hesiod's Cosmogony.

Hesiod's Cosmogony is a creation myth explaining the universe's origins and the birth of the gods. It is a tale that has captured peoples' imaginations for centuries and continues to influence today's Hellenism belief system. Here's how it goes:

In the beginning, there was Chaos, a formless and empty void. From Chaos emerged two primal beings: Gaia, the Earth, and her firstborn, Uranus (known as Ouranos), the "starry heaven." Gaia had many children, including the Titans, who were the first gods. The Titans included powerful figures like Cronus, Rhea, and Oceanus.

However, Uranus was a cruel and tyrannical father, and his children were unhappy with him. Cronus, the youngest of the Titans, eventually rebelled against his father and overthrew him with the help of his mother, Gaia. After becoming the new ruler of the gods, Cronus became even more tyrannical than Uranus. He swallowed his children to prevent them from challenging him.

However, one of Cronus' children, Zeus, was spared from this fate. He grew up in secret and eventually overthrew his father, becoming the king of the gods. With the help of his siblings, the Olympians, Zeus defeated the Titans and became the undisputed ruler of the cosmos."

The story of Hesiod's Cosmogony provides a fascinating explanation for the universe's origins and is crucial in shaping the Hellenism belief system. The myth teaches the importance of order, balance, and harmony in the world. As the personification of these ideals, the gods serve as guides for mortals to follow in their daily lives.

Gods and Goddesses

Each god and goddess in Greek mythology had a unique role and attribute reflecting different aspects of the human experience. Together, they formed a complex and interconnected Pantheon to explain natural phenomena, human emotions, and the complexities of human relationships.

1. Zeus

Zeus was the king of the gods and the god of the sky and thunder. He was known for his power, strength, and wisdom. He was often depicted as a strong, muscular man with a beard, holding a lightning bolt. He was married to his sister, Hera, who was one of the twelve Olympian gods. Zeus was known for his numerous affairs and had many children with mortal and immortal women. He was known for his role in enforcing justice and maintaining order in the world.

2. Hera

Hera was the queen of the gods and the goddess of marriage, childbirth, and family. She was often depicted as a beautiful woman wearing a crown or headdress, holding a lotus flower or a scepter. She was fiercely loyal to her husband, Zeus, but was known for her jealousy toward his numerous affairs. She was a protector of women and children and was associated with the domestic realm. Her children included

Hephaestus, the god of fire and craftsmanship, and Ares, the god of war.

3. Poseidon

Poseidon was the god of the sea, earthquakes, and horses. He was often depicted as a muscular man with a trident, riding a chariot pulled by horses. He was known for his temper and was often associated with destruction and creation. He was one of the three brothers who divided the world among themselves, with Zeus receiving the sky, Hades receiving the underworld, and Poseidon receiving the sea.

4. Demeter

Demeter was the goddess of agriculture and fertility. She was often depicted as a mature woman, carrying a sheaf of wheat or a cornucopia. She was Zeus' sister and the mother of Persephone, who was abducted by Hades and taken to the underworld. Demeter's grief at the loss of her daughter was said to have caused the change of seasons, with the barren winter months representing the time when Persephone was in the underworld.

5. Athena

Athena was the goddess of wisdom, strategy, and warfare. She was often depicted as a strong, beautiful woman wearing a helmet and carrying a shield and spear. She was born fully grown and armored from her father's head, Zeus. She was a virgin goddess associated with the arts, sciences, civic duty, and justice.

6. Apollo

Apollo was the god of music, poetry, prophecy, and healing. He was the son of Zeus and Leto and the twin brother of Artemis. He was known for his musical skills and was often depicted with a lyre or a bow and arrows. Apollo was associated with the Sun and was believed to drive his chariot across the sky daily. He was often consulted as an oracle at the temple of Delphi and believed to have the power to heal.

7. Artemis

Artemis was the goddess of the hunt, the wilderness, childbirth, and virginity. She was the daughter of Zeus and Leto and the twin sister of Apollo. Artemis was often depicted with a bow and arrows and was known for her skill as a hunter. She was associated with the Moon and was believed to help women during childbirth. Artemis was often revered as a protector of young women and a champion of virginity.

8. Demeter

Demeter was the goddess of agriculture, fertility, and the harvest. She was the daughter of Cronus and Rhea and the sister of Zeus. Demeter was often depicted with a sheaf of wheat or corn. She was revered as a protector of farmers and those who worked the land. She was associated with the seasons and believed to have the power to bring about the seasons' changes.

9. Dionysus

Dionysus was the god of wine, fertility, and theater. He was the son of Zeus and Semele and was often depicted holding a wine cup and surrounded by revelers. Dionysus was associated with the wild and was often worshiped in rituals that involved wine and ecstatic dancing. He was known for his ability to inspire creativity and was revered as a patron of the arts.

10. Hades

Hades was the god of the underworld and the dead. He was the son of Cronus and Rhea and the brother of Zeus and Poseidon. Hades ruled over the dead and was often depicted as a dark and foreboding figure. He was associated with wealth and riches, as the underground minerals were believed to be his domain. Mortals feared Hades, as death was seen as a final and irreversible separation from the world of the living.

11. Hephaestus

Hephaestus was the Greek god of fire, metalworking, and craftsmanship. He was the son of Zeus and Hera. Hephaestus was known for his exceptional skill in crafting weapons, armor, and other objects made of metal. Despite his important role in Greek mythology, he was often portrayed as physically unattractive, with a limp or deformed leg. According to stories, his mother cast him out of Olympus because of his appearance. He landed on Lemnos Island, where he set up his forge. Despite his physical limitations, Hephaestus was highly respected by the other gods for his skill and creativity. He was said to have crafted many of the most famous weapons and artifacts in Greek mythology, including the lightning bolts wielded by Zeus, the shield of Achilles, and the chariot of the Sun.

12. Hermes

Hermes was one of the twelve Olympian gods in Greek mythology. He was the son of Zeus and the Pleiad Maia and was known as the messenger of the gods. Hermes was a multifaceted god associated with many responsibilities, including commerce, thieves, travelers, athletes, and diplomacy. He was typically depicted as a youthful and athletic figure, often wearing a broad-brimmed hat and carrying a caduceus, a winged staff with two snakes wrapped around it. He was known for his speed and agility and was often called upon by the other gods to deliver messages or perform tasks. In addition to his role as a messenger, Hermes was the god of thieves and commerce. He was believed to be the protector of merchants and travelers and was associated with the boundaries between different places and realms.

Festivals and Celebrations

The Hellenic calendar was filled with numerous celebrations and rituals honoring the gods and goddesses of Greek mythology. These events served as religious observances and important social and cultural occasions that united communities.

One of the most well-known celebrations was the Olympic Games, held every four years in honor of Zeus. The games were a time for athletic competition and included events such as running, jumping, and wrestling. The winners were celebrated as heroes, and the games were a way to promote unity and peace among the city-states of ancient Greece.

Another important ritual was the Eleusinian Mysteries, held in honor of the goddess Demeter and her daughter Persephone. The mysteries were secret rituals only open to those who had been initiated into the cult of Demeter. The rituals were said to reveal the secrets of life, death, and the afterlife. They were believed to bring spiritual purification and enlightenment to those who participated.

The Dionysian festivals, held in honor of the god Dionysus, were another important event in the Hellenic calendar. These festivals were marked by wild and raucous music, dance, and feasting celebrations. The followers of Dionysus believed that by engaging in these ecstatic rituals, they could experience divine communion with the god and achieve a state of transcendence and spiritual liberation.

In addition to the traditional celebrations and rituals, modern-day festivals and events are inspired by Hellenic polytheism. These events are often organized by modern-day Hellenic communities and serve to honor the gods and goddesses of Greek mythology. One event is the Hellenic Revival Festival, which occurs in Greece annually. This festival features music, dance, and theater performances celebrating the Hellenic heritage of Greece and pays tribute to the ancient gods and goddesses.

Hellenic Ritual

Hellenism places great importance on the practice of rituals and ceremonies as ways of honoring the gods and maintaining a connection with the divine. These rituals often involve offering sacrifices, including food, drink, or animals. Temples and other sacred sites are important to Hellenic practitioners and where the gods can be contacted and worshiped. These rituals and offerings help reinforce the interconnectedness of the natural world and the relationship between humans and the gods.

One simple Hellenic ritual you can perform in your space is the Libation Ritual. This ritual involves pouring a small amount of wine, olive oil, or honey as an offering to the gods and goddesses.

Materials:
- A small bowl or cup for the libation
- Wine, olive oil, or honey
- A candle or incense for lighting
- Any offerings or symbols you would like to include, such as flowers, herbs, or statues of the gods and goddesses

Preparation:
- Set up a sacred space in your home or outdoor area, using symbols or objects meaningful to you.
- Light the candle or incense to create a peaceful and focused atmosphere.
- Choose which deity or deities you want to honor and prepare a small offering of wine, olive oil, or honey.

Ritual:
1. Stand before your altar or sacred space and take a deep breath, centering yourself in the present moment.
2. Light the candle or incense, and offer a prayer or invocation to the gods and goddesses, inviting their presence and blessing on your ritual.
3. Pour a small amount of the libation into the bowl or cup, and speak a few words of gratitude or intention to the deity you

are honoring.
4. Raise the bowl or cup in your hands, and offer the libation as an offering to the deity. As you pour the liquid, you can say a prayer, chant a hymn, or simply offer your thoughts and intentions.
5. After the libation is poured, offer other offerings or symbols, such as flowers, herbs, or incense, and meditate or reflect on your connection to the deity and its teachings.
6. When you are ready, extinguish the candle or incense, and give thanks to the deity for their presence and blessings.

Safety and ethical considerations:
- Always be respectful and mindful when performing any spiritual practice.
- Use caution when working with candles or incense, and ensure they are not left unattended.
- Use only a small amount of alcohol if choosing wine for the libation, and avoid drinking excess alcohol during the ritual.

Greek Polytheism and Spirituality offer a unique and compelling view of the world that has influenced countless cultures throughout history. From the complex relationships between the gods and goddesses to the importance of music, dance, and feasting, this belief system offers a rich and diverse array of traditions that continue to inspire today. Whether you are an adherent of Paganism or merely interested in exploring new spiritual practices, the rituals and celebrations of Hellenism offer a powerful way to connect with the divine and find meaning in your life.

Chapter 7: Wicca: A Neopagan View

Paganism has been around for centuries, encompassing diverse spiritual practices and beliefs honoring the natural world and its cycles. However, it is hard not to immediately think of Wicca when you think of modern Paganism. Wicca emerged in the early 1950s as a new form of Paganism, drawing inspiration from ancient pagan practices and beliefs. Despite being relatively young compared to other pagan paths, Wicca has grown in popularity over the years and is a prominent and influential spirituality in modern times.

But what is Wicca? How does it differ from other forms of neopaganism? As you explore the world of Wicca and modern neopaganism, you will uncover a vibrant and diverse spiritual landscape honoring nature's sacredness and life's cycles. In particular, Wicca draws upon ancient pagan and magical practices while incorporating newer beliefs and ideas. From the Wiccan Rede to the various traditions and festivals, the Wiccan path is intriguing and complex. While often used interchangeably, not all neopagans are Wiccans, and vice versa. So, dive into the nuances and differences between Wicca and neopaganism, and discover what makes each path unique.

Wiccan traditions and spells honor nature.
https://unsplash.com/photos/-AfRBlhuaHE?utm_source=unsplash&utm_medium=referral&utm_content=creditShareLink

Origins of Wicca and Neopaganism

Wicca and neopaganism have their roots in ancient pagan practices, which were widespread throughout Europe before the spread of Christianity. The rise of Christianity led to the suppression and persecution of Paganism, but the beliefs and practices survived and continued to evolve in secret. In the early 20th century, interest in Paganism resurged, particularly with the growth of the occult and esoteric movements. In the 1950s, Gerald Gardner, an Englishman initiated into a coven of witches, publicly promoted Wicca as a new form of Paganism. It marked the birth of Wicca as a distinct spiritual path, although it drew heavily on ancient pagan beliefs and practices.

On the other hand, neopaganism refers to a broader umbrella of modern pagan paths that draw inspiration from various ancient traditions. It includes traditions such as Druidry, Asatru, and Hellenismos. Neopaganism emerged in the 1960s and 1970s. It is characterized by a strong focus on ecological and environmental concerns and a rejection of patriarchy and other hierarchical structures.

Comparison between Wicca and Neopaganism

Wicca is often associated with neopaganism. However, it is important to understand that they are not synonymous. While all Wiccans are neopagans to some degree, not all neopagans are Wiccans. Wicca is a specific neopaganism tradition with its own beliefs, practices, and rituals.

One of the key differences between Wicca and other neopagan traditions is the emphasis on witchcraft and magic. While many neopagan traditions incorporate magical practices, Wicca strongly emphasizes magic as a central aspect of its practice. Another difference is their use of covens. While some neopagan traditions practice in groups, Wicca is known for using covens typically led by a high priestess or priest.

The Wiccan Belief System

Wicca is a modern pagan religion with roots in ancient pagan practices. It is characterized by its reverence for nature, belief in a divine feminine and masculine figure, and use of magic and ritual. Here are some key points in the Wiccan belief system:

- **Polytheism:** Wiccans believe in the existence of multiple gods and goddesses, each with their distinct personalities and areas of influence. These deities are often associated with natural elements and forces like the Sun, Moon, and Earth.
- **Divine polarity:** Wiccans believe in the concept of divine polarity, which posits that the universe is made up of two complementary forces, the feminine and the masculine. These forces are often represented by a goddess and a god, respectively.
- **Reverence for nature:** Wiccans believe in the inherent sacredness of nature and seek to live in harmony with the natural world. They often celebrate the changing seasons and cycles of the Moon through ritual and ceremony.
- **The power of intention:** Wiccans believe that thoughts and intentions have the power to shape the world. It is often expressed through magic and rituals.

The Wiccan Rede and Its Importance

The Wiccan Rede is a statement of ethics central to the Wiccan belief system. It states, "An it harm none, do what ye will," meaning as long as your actions do not cause harm to others, you are free to act in accordance with your own will. This Rede is often interpreted as a call for personal responsibility and ethical behavior. The Wiccan Rede is often used as a guiding principle in decision-making and to promote positive actions and discourage negative ones.

The Wiccan Rede is not a commandment but rather a guideline for ethical behavior. It is up to the individual Wiccan to interpret the Rede and apply it to their lives. Some Wiccans interpret the Rede to mean they should avoid causing harm to any living being, while others take a more nuanced approach and understand that sometimes harm is necessary to protect themselves or others.

The Wiccan Rede is often viewed as a way to promote harmony and balance in the world. Wiccans believe their actions have a ripple effect affecting the world around them, and the Rede is a way to promote positive energy and discourage negative energy. By following the Rede, Wiccans can live in accordance with their beliefs and promote a more peaceful and harmonious world.

The Role of Magic in Wicca

Magic is an integral part of the Wiccan belief system. Wiccans believe that through ritual and intention, they can tap into the universe's power and manifest their desires, often done through spells designed to direct energy toward a specific goal. Wiccans also believe in karma, which states that the energy you put into the world will return to you. Therefore, magic is seen as a way to promote positive change in the world while taking responsibility for your actions.

Wiccan Traditions

Wicca is a highly diverse religion with many different Wiccan traditions existing today. Each tradition has its unique practices, beliefs, and rituals, and it can be difficult for outsiders to understand the differences. This section provides an overview of some of the most popular Wiccan traditions and explains the differences.

Gardnerian Wicca

One of the most well-known Wiccan traditions is Gardnerian Wicca, which Gerald Gardner founded in the 1950s. This tradition emphasizes the worship of the Horned God and the Mother Goddess and strongly emphasizes initiation and coven membership. Gardnerian Wicca is a highly structured tradition, and its members are expected to follow specific rules and practices.

- Gardnerian Wiccan rituals are typically held in a circle, representing the sacred space between the physical and the spiritual worlds. The circle is cast using various tools and symbols, like a wand or a sword, and the four elements (earth, air, fire, and water) are called upon to protect the space and those within it.
- The ritual is usually led by a High Priestess or High Priest, assisted by other coven members. The ritual can include elements such as chanting, drumming, dancing, and meditation. Coven members can take on specific roles during the ritual, like calling upon a particular element or deity.
- One of the key elements of Gardnerian Wiccan rituals is using the Great Rite. This rite involves a symbolic union of the Horned God and the Mother Goddess, representing the union of masculine and feminine energies. In some rituals, this involves a ritual blade (the athame) and a chalice of wine or other liquid.
- Another important aspect of Gardnerian Wiccan rituals is using magical energy to manifest desires or intentions. It involves spells, visualizations, or other techniques to focus and direct energy toward a particular goal.
- At the end of the ritual, the circle is opened, and the elements are thanked and released. Coven members usually share food and drink as a symbol of community and fellowship.

Alexandrian Wicca

Another popular Wiccan tradition is Alexandrian Wicca, founded by Alex Sanders in the 1960s. This tradition is similar to Gardnerian Wicca in many ways, but it places a greater emphasis on ceremonial magic and ritual. Alexandrian Wiccans often use various tools and symbols in their rituals, including swords, chalices, and wands.

- One of the key differences between Gardnerian and Alexandrian Wicca is the focus on using ceremonial magic in Alexandrian Wicca. While both traditions use ritual and magic to connect with the divine, Alexandrian Wiccans greatly emphasize using ceremonial magic techniques, such as ritual drama and specific correspondences and symbols.
- Alexandrian Wiccan rituals are similar in structure to Gardnerian rituals in terms of using a sacred circle, calling upon the elements and deities, and using the Great Rite. However, Alexandrian Wicca incorporates additional elements, such as ritual drama, trance work, and specific correspondences and symbols to focus and direct magical energy.
- Another key aspect of Alexandrian Wicca is the degree system, which consists of three degrees of initiation. As with Gardnerian Wicca, initiation into each degree involves specific teachings and practices, and initiates are expected to progress through the degrees to deepen their understanding and connection with the divine.
- Some other notable aspects of Alexandrian Wicca include the Rose Cross symbol, the emphasis on ceremonial magic, and the focus on the degree system as a means of spiritual growth and development.

Eclectic Wicca

Eclectic Wicca is a more modern tradition that emerged in the 1970s. This tradition is less structured than Gardnerian or Alexandrian Wicca and allows greater flexibility and individualism. Eclectic Wiccans often draw on various traditions and practices and create their rituals and practices based on their personal beliefs and experiences.

- Eclectic Wicca is a non-initiatory form of Wicca often practiced by individuals not drawn to any specific tradition or coven. It is a highly individualized Wicca allowing practitioners to pick and choose elements from various traditions and incorporate them into their practice.
- As the name suggests, eclectic Wicca blends different Wiccan traditions and other spiritual and religious practices. Practitioners of eclectic Wicca often create their own rituals, spells, and correspondences based on what resonates with them personally.

- Since eclectic Wicca is so personalized, the tradition has no initiation process or hierarchy. Many eclectic Wiccans practice alone, but some join groups or covens that are also eclectic in nature.
- One of the key aspects of eclectic Wicca is the emphasis on personal responsibility and the idea that the practitioner is the ultimate authority in their spiritual practice. So, there is no single "right" way to practice eclectic Wicca, and practitioners are encouraged to experiment and find what works best for them.
- Eclectic Wiccans draw inspiration from numerous sources, including different Wiccan traditions, other pagan and earth-based spiritualities, and even non-spiritual sources, like literature or pop culture. It makes eclectic Wicca a highly adaptable and flexible tradition that can be tailored to meet the needs and interests of individual practitioners.

There are many other Wiccan traditions, including Dianic Wicca, which places a greater emphasis on worshipping the goddess; Celtic Wicca, which draws on the traditions of ancient Celtic cultures; and Feri Wicca, which emphasizes ecstatic and trance-like experiences.

While each Wiccan tradition has its unique practices and beliefs, there are many similarities between them. Most Wiccans believe in worshiping a horned god and a mother goddess, and many strongly emphasize rituals and magic. However, the differences between traditions can be significant, and it is important for Wiccans to carefully consider their beliefs and values before choosing a particular tradition to follow.

Wiccan Festivals

Wiccan festivals, known as sabbats, are integral to the Wiccan belief system and calendar. Eight major sabbats are celebrated throughout the year, each marking an important point in the agricultural cycle and the changing seasons.

1. Samhain

Samhain is celebrated on October 31st and is considered the Wiccan New Year. It is a time to honor the ancestors, remember loved ones who have passed away, and let go of things no longer serving you. This festival is often associated with divination. It is believed the veil between the living and the dead is the thinnest on this day. People would leave food and drink offerings on their doorsteps to honor and welcome their ancestors or set a place at the table for them. This practice resembles the Day of the Dead celebrations in Mexico and other Latin American countries. As divination was a significant part of Samhain celebrations, many people believed that on this night, they could communicate with their ancestors' spirits and receive their messages and guidance. They would use divination tools like tarot cards, scrying mirrors, and Ogham staves to connect with the spirit world.

2. Yule

Yule is celebrated on the winter solstice, usually around December 21st. It marks the shortest day and longest night of the year. It is a time to celebrate the return of the Sun and the lengthening of the days. Yule is often associated with a god's birth and the Earth's renewal. Many modern pagans and Wiccans celebrate Yule as one of the eight sabbats, during which they gather in groups to perform rituals and cast spells or celebrate in a more solitary way. Whatever their approach, Yule is a time to honor the cycles of nature and celebrate the light that shines within everyone.

3. Imbolc

Imbolc is celebrated on February 1st or 2nd and marks the beginning of spring. It is a time to honor the goddess Brigid, who is associated with healing, creativity, and inspiration. Imbolc is often celebrated with purification rituals and lighting candles to represent the Sun's returning light. In addition to purification rituals and candle lighting, Imbolc is celebrated through feasting and exchanging gifts. Some traditional foods associated with the festival include dairy products, like milk and cheese, and bread and cakes.

4. Ostara

Ostara is celebrated on the spring equinox, usually around March 20th. It marks the balance between light and dark and the beginning of the planting season. Ostara is often associated with the goddess Eostre, who is associated with fertility, growth, and new beginnings. Ostara is a time to celebrate the power of the natural world and the interconnectedness of all things. Some common rituals practiced during Ostara include planting seeds, creating springtime crafts, and decorating eggs, symbolic of new life and rebirth.

5. Beltane

Beltane is celebrated on May 1st and marks the beginning of summer. It is a time to celebrate the union of the god and goddess and the Earth's fertility and abundance. Beltane is often celebrated with Maypole dances, flower crowns, and bonfires. Another key aspect of Beltane is lighting bonfires, which are seen as a way to purify and renew the land's energy. The fires are associated with the idea of transformation and crossing boundaries as people leap over the flames to symbolize their willingness to embrace change and growth.

6. Litha

Litha is celebrated on the summer solstice, usually around June 21st. It marks the longest day and shortest night of the year and a time to celebrate the Sun's power and the Earth's abundance. Litha is often associated with the god Lugh, who is associated with skills, craftsmanship, and creativity. At Litha, practitioners celebrate through numerous rituals and activities, including bonfires, feasts, and flower wreaths. Some people choose to spend time outdoors, soaking up the energy of the Sun and connecting with the natural world.

7. Lammas/Lughnasadh

Lammas or Lughnasadh is celebrated on August 1st and marks the beginning of the harvest season. It is a time to honor the god Lugh, associated with the grain harvest, and the goddess as the mother of the harvest. Lammas is often celebrated by baking bread and sharing a communal meal. Another key theme of Lammas is sacrifice. The harvest's first fruits are offered as a sacrifice to the gods in recognition of their providing for the people. This sacrifice is seen as a way to ensure continued abundance and prosperity in the coming year.

8. Mabon

Mabon is celebrated on the autumn equinox, usually around September 21st. It marks the balance between light and dark and the second harvest of the year. Mabon is often associated with the god Mabon, associated with rebirth and the turning of the seasons. The festivities include activities reflecting the abundance of the harvest, such as apple picking, wine-making, and creating harvest-themed crafts. Acts of charity and giving are common, recognizing that the blessings received are meant to be shared. As the Sun sets on Mabon, candles are lit, and people gather around the fire to share stories and reflect on the cycles of life and the passage of time.

Each festival is celebrated with specific rituals and practices designed to honor the specific energy and themes of the sabbat. These include offerings to the gods and goddesses, casting spells, lighting candles or fires, creating altars and sacred spaces, and sharing food and drink.

The importance of these festivals lies in their connection to the natural world and the changing of the seasons. By honoring the cycles of the Earth and the energy of each season, Wiccans believe they can cultivate a deeper connection to the natural world and the divine. These festivals serve as a time to come together as a community and celebrate shared beliefs.

Wiccan Structure and Roles

Wicca is a decentralized religion with no central authority or hierarchy. Its structure is based on covens, small groups of Wiccans who gather to practice their craft. Various roles and responsibilities are usually assigned to its members within a coven.

At the top of the Wiccan hierarchy is the High Priestess or High Priest, who is the leader of the coven. The High Priestess or High Priest is responsible for leading rituals, teaching new members, and guiding the spiritual development of the coven. They are responsible for maintaining the coven's traditions and ensuring that it adheres to Wiccan ethics and principles.

Below the High Priestess or High Priest are the coven members. Coven members are typically initiated into the coven and expected to participate in activities such as rituals and meetings. They can take on specific roles within the coven, like the coven's secretary or treasurer.

In addition to these roles, various degrees of initiation are within Wicca. These degrees signify a Wiccan's knowledge and experience level within the religion. First-degree Wiccans are typically new to the religion and have not yet been initiated into a coven. Second-degree Wiccans have been initiated into a coven and have a deeper understanding of Wiccan practices and beliefs. Third-degree Wiccans are considered High Priests or High Priestesses and have the knowledge and experience necessary to lead their covens.

Simple Full Moon Ritual

The objective of this ritual is to honor the full Moon and connect with its energy. Through this ritual, you have the opportunity to deepen your understanding and appreciation of the natural cycles and rhythms of the Earth and the Moon and align yourself with the powerful energies during the full Moon phase.

Materials:
- A candle (preferably white or silver)
- Matches or a lighter
- A piece of paper and a pen
- A small dish with water
- Any additional ritual tools (optional)

Instructions:
1. Choose a quiet, outdoor space where you can see the full Moon. Alternatively, you can set up an altar indoors with a representation of the Moon, like a picture or a statue.
2. Begin by grounding and centering yourself. Take a few deep breaths and visualize yourself becoming fully present in the moment.
3. Light the candle and hold it up to the Moon. Say a simple blessing, such as "Blessed be the light of the full Moon."
4. Write down whatever you want to release or let go of on the piece of paper and the intentions or goals you want to manifest in the upcoming month. Fold the paper and place it on the dish of water.
5. Hold your hands over the dish and say, *"I release what no longer serves me and open myself to new opportunities and growth."* Visualize the water absorbing the negative energy or unwanted thoughts and feelings.
6. Take a moment to feel the full Moon's energy and connect with your intuition and inner wisdom.
7. When you are ready, blow out the candle and say, *"So, mote it be,"* meaning *"Let it be so."*
8. Dispose of the paper and water in a way that is safe and respectful to the environment.

9. Close the ritual by thanking the deities or spirits you called upon and thanking yourself for taking the time to honor the full Moon.

Despite being thousands of years old, Wicca and neopaganism remain relevant spiritual practices for many individuals in modern times. As society becomes more disconnected from nature and traditional spirituality, many people are turning to Wicca and neopaganism as a way to reconnect with the natural world and their spirituality. Wicca and neopaganism allow individuals to create their own spiritual practices based on their beliefs and values. This way, Wicca and neopaganism remain important and relevant practices for many individuals in the modern world.

Chapter 8: Applying Your Pagan Beliefs to Daily Life

This final chapter takes a practical approach to what it means to be a modern pagan and how to go about it in your everyday life. This chapter will provide instructions on how to find a deity to work with, set up an altar, celebrate pagan holidays, start a journal or grimoire, connect with other pagans, and more.

Finding Your Patron or Matron Deity

While having a patron or matron deity is optional, they can help you find your path by guiding you in the right direction. They can protect and empower you during your pagan work (magical or otherwise) and help you heal if needed. However, if you decide to find a patron or matron deity, you should start by exploring yourself. Remember, the power comes from within you. Any energy you receive from a divine being or nature will only amplify the power you already have. So, the best way to find the deity to empower you is to look for those whose correspondents resonate with you.

Reading about deities you find interesting may help you connect with them.
https://unsplash.com/photos/OfaDD5o8hpk?utm_source=unsplash&utm_medium=referral&utm_content=creditShareLink

Research the deities you find interesting. While reading about each particular god or goddess, listen to your intuition. If you feel particularly drawn to one, dive deeper into their backgrounds, history, myths, and correspondences. Learn how other modern-day practitioners work with the god or goddess. If you're absolutely certain about wanting to work with a particular deity, contact them by dedicating a prayer to them. Alternatively, you can light a candle and gaze into its flames while chanting the deity's name. However, sometimes simply showing interest in them will earn their attention, and they will contact you.

If the deity you have chosen doesn't communicate with you right away, don't worry. They might feel you don't need their help at that moment. Or, it could be that you don't know how to recognize or decipher their signs yet. While you can express how you would like to be contacted, some deities have their own ways. For example, if you've addressed them in prayer before sleeping, they might approach you in your dreams.

Consider holding an introductory ritual if you struggle to connect with your chosen matron or patron deity. Here is how to do it:

1. Dedicate a small altar to them, and adorn it with their correspondences and symbols.

2. Light a candle in their name, call on them, and introduce yourself.
3. State your name and your intention of forming a relationship with them.
4. Express your gratitude for any blessing you might receive in the future.
5. Repeat if needed in a few days.

When you start working with your matron or patron, feel free to set boundaries for your relationship. As with any relationship, working with a pagan deity is a two-way street. You should count on their blessing just as much as they should count on you honoring and celebrating them. They should listen to you just as much as you should listen to them. If the deity you made contact with turns out to be a bad match for you, feel free to end your relationship. Remember, you don't have to settle for the first deity you feel drawn to, nor must you keep working with the same matron or patron deity all your life. So many options are available, and you might need different assistance at the various stages of your life.

Setting Up Your Altar

While having an altar isn't mandatory in pagan practice, it can help you channel your energy into your intention. It helps link with a deity, spirit, and your spirituality. Here is how to set up a simple pagan altar.

Choose the Placement

Many pagans practice outdoors, but if you prefer to do it indoors, feel free to place your altar inside your home. Either way, it should be where you can work without distractions and where it won't bother you or anyone else living in your home. Most practitioners who use indoor altars opt for placing them in their bedrooms as this is the most secluded room in a house.

You can use an old table or dresser as the base of your altar, you'll cover it anyway, so it won't matter how it looks. Or, if you have limited space, you can always set it up on your dresser, bookcase, or windowsill. A naturally flat surface, like a large tree trunk, will work if you're setting up an outside altar.

Consider the Direction

The direction you set up your altar facing depends on your practice, preferences, and available space. Suppose you're working with limited space or aren't sure which direction would fit your purpose, create an east-facing altar. In that case, this is the direction of the rising sun, which is powerful in many pagan practices.

Decide on the Style

The style of your altar depends on the pagan path you follow. If you wish to dedicate it to a specific entity or holiday, the style will be influenced by their associations. Or, if you haven't decided on a particular spiritual path or purpose for your altar, go with your gut feelings. Let your intuition decide on the style; it might reveal the course you should follow.

Choose the Adornments

Use their association and representatives if working with a particular deity (or planning to work with one). If you have a matron or patron deity, place their symbols on the center of your altar. If you're working with your ancestors, use their representation or their personal items if you have any. If you want to empower yourself, include your personal items.

Other suggested items to place on the altar:
- Divination tools
- Symbols of protection
- Crystals
- Wands and athames
- Grimoire or book of shadows
- Candles
- The representation of the four elements
- Loose herbs
- Talismans or amulets

Celebrating Esbats and Sabbats

Pagans worldwide celebrate esbats (Moon rituals) and Sabbats (seasonal festivities) in a myriad of ways. Some traditions are community-based, while others are highly personal. As a beginner, you should focus on establishing personal traditions for these holidays. It will help you understand their significance and inspire you to dedicate more time to them. Here are suggested practices to celebrate pagan holidays.

Decorating

Nearly all pagan rituals and ceremonies performed at esbats and sabbats use candles. Decorating candles is a great way to celebrate any pagan holiday. Use colors, herbs, and other materials associated with the holiday. You can let your creativity loose and make as many candles as you wish. You'll use candles for your altar, as adornments for your home, or as gifts.

You can make decorations with flowers and other elements of nature. Whichever material you use should be associated with the specific holiday. For example, some herbs have protective abilities, and making a wreath from them for your front door can be an excellent complementary practice for protection spells and rituals.

Preparing Tools

Some pagans prefer to prepare their own oils, herbal blends, symbols, representations, and other tools in their practice. While you can purchase your tools pre-made, making them can be satisfying and spiritually uplifting, especially if you're preparing for a sacred day or holiday. You'll have a more powerful connection with your tools, as they'll be automatically charged with your energy.

Cleansing

Whichever esbat or sabbat you're preparing for, it doesn't hurt to cleanse yourself and your property from negative influences. Each holiday marks a momentous event on a pagan calendar and represents the beginning of a new period. It's always better to start a new period with a clean slate or, better yet, be empowered with positive energy. Here are suggestions on how to cleanse yourself and your home:

- Smudging
- Incense
- Cleansing bath
- Sprinkling salt
- Basking in moonlight
- Using a cleansing spell
- Asking a deity to help you cleanse
- Using a cleaning talisman or pouch made of herbs
- Drinking herbal tea
- Walking in nature

- Standing in sunlight
- Surrounding yourself with houseplants

Preparing Meals

Whether you celebrate an esbat or sabbat with a large community, your friends, your family, or alone, preparing meals associated with that holiday is a fantastic way to get into the spirit. Look into what other modern practitioners of your chosen pagan path recommend preparing for a particular holiday, and pick your favorite recipes. Even if you live with other non-pagan family members, you can still ask them to help you prepare the meals. It can be a terrific activity for families with children as they usually like learning and doing something new.

Creating a Logbook, Journal, or Grimoire

Recording your practice is a great way to monitor the progress of your spiritual journey. If you're just starting, create a logbook of rituals and acts you've performed throughout the day, week, or month. It will help you keep track of the planned tasks and ensure you don't forget to implement them regularly. The more pagan practices you incorporate into your schedule, the closer you discover your spiritual path.

Start a journal if you practice divination, attempt to communicate with your spiritual guides, or want a more detailed characterization of your practices. Unlike a logbook (which only has data about specific tasks), a journal can contain the signs and messages you've received, your emotions regarding specific tools, or anything else you might want to document along your journey.

If you also practice witchcraft, you can start a grimoire. A grimoire is a book that keeps track of magical practices. It can contain correspondence of deities and ancestors, sabbats, esbats, and other sacred days you celebrate. Or your preferred ways to cast spells, specific spells and rituals you've done, divination methods, astrological correspondences, herbs and recipes for healing agents, and crystals. It can include topics you feel inspired by or want to learn.

Whether you create a logbook, journal, or grimoire, remember to keep it safe. You have a personal connection to it, and any energy the book picks up can affect you. Cleanse it often and consecrate it if necessary.

Connecting with Other Pagans

Connecting to other pagan groups and communities is a great way to gain more knowledge and understanding of a particular spiritual path. In these modern times, there are plenty of ways to find like-minded people near you or even on the other side of the world. If you don't mind the distance or just looking for advice, look for pagan groups on social media sites and forums. Whichever pagan path you wish to follow, you'll find the group that suits your needs.

If you prefer to find people you can meet, exchange experiences with, and celebrate sabbats, esbats, and other pagan holidays, or worship deities together, look around in your area. Start with occult bookshops, as these typically have posted notices of other pagans looking for communities or pagan communities looking to gather new members.

Whichever way you get in touch with other pagans, feel free to share your spiritual journey with them, no matter how short. Maybe your experience will help someone struggling to find their path or has veered off an already established path and looking for their way back.

Pagan Life To-Dos

Part of embarking on a pagan path is to cater to your spiritual needs. Fortunately, many ways exist to incorporate simple daily pagan rituals without affecting your schedule. Following a to-do list will help you, and you don't have to check every item on the list every day. Feel free to pick and choose a few that can fit into your routine. The overall goal is to create a habit of daily pagan rituals to help you get closer to the pagan lifestyle.

Here is the checklist of pagan rituals:

- Light a candle. You can say a quick prayer of gratitude to your matron or patron deity, ancestors, or other spiritual guides with whom you have been working.
- Make offerings to a deity. You can keep this ritual as simple as you want. For example, you can offer them a cup of coffee or water or share a meal with them.
- Make offerings to your ancestors. Remember to offer their favorite items.
- Rise to greet the Sun. The Sun is fundamental in most pagan traditions. Spending a couple of minutes basking in sunlight

after you wake up can help you take advantage of its energy.
- Do yoga. Even one or two positions daily will do wonders for your spiritual life.
- Go for a walk (preferably in nature) to reconnect with nature's power. During lunch hour, 10 minutes will do the trick. However, you should aim for regular walks outside.
- Try dream journaling. Set a journal at your bedside, so you can record your dreams as soon as you wake up. It can help you connect and communicate with spirits, deities, and your intuition.
- Mediate. Daily meditation is recommended for most spiritual seekers. Whether you listen to a guided meditation or let your intuition lead you, it doesn't matter.
- Pay attention to nature. Be more vigilant of your surroundings to notice the little signs and omens nature sends you.
- Light incense. Similarly to candlelight, the incense's scent is soothing and grounding. It creates the perfect atmosphere for mediation, rituals, and magical work.
- Read a spiritual book. Even if you have only 15 minutes to set aside for reading, use it to learn more about the spiritual path you've chosen to follow.
- Spend time with your pets. If you have pets, spending time with them would be the perfect pagan way to honor nature.
- Light a red candle in the kitchen. This ritual honors your ancestors and symbolizes the hearth (fireplace), which most modern homes don't have. However, it was indispensable in pagan traditions.
- Cleanse yourself and your area with smoke. Some pagans call it a smudging ritual. It involves lighting a bundle of dried herbs and enveloping yourself and the space or object you want to cleanse from bad energies in their smoke.
- Spend time with your family. This is another essential pagan ritual recommended daily. Even if you have 10-15 minutes to show how much you care, do it.
- Write a book of shadows or grimoire. This book can help you monitor your progress on your spiritual journey and learn to follow the pagan path you find fulfilling.

- Wear a crystal. You can wear jewelry with crystal in the morning or put the stone in your pocket or bag. Either way, if you have charged it with positive energy, it will protect you and enhance your power throughout the day.
- Start and tend to a garden. Whether you have a place for a few pots on your windowsill or a full-size garden in your backyard, tending to your garden is a very satisfying pagan ritual.
- Exercise. With the modern, sedentary lifestyle, exercising can be a pagan ritual. It can help you remember all your ancestors' physical work to sustain their families. Without their efforts, you wouldn't be where you are.
- Drink herbal tea. Brewing herbal tea in the morning and sipping it is a great way to slow down and prepare for your upcoming spiritual challenges.
- Read a card or rune. If you practice divination (or want to enhance your spirituality), pick a card or rune every morning and contemplate its meaning.
- Use herbs for cooking. Herbs have incredible healing properties, and your ancestors knew this. They used them in their daily lives, and so can you.
- Freshen up your altar or shrine. Check your sacred place daily for ashes, dust, and debris, and clean it if necessary. Replace your offerings (especially if you have food items) or exchange them for different ones.
- Gaze at the Moon. Just as sitting in the sunlight can help you recharge your energies, so can gazing at the Moon. You can go outside when the sky is clear or sit at an open window.
- Plan the next sabbat or esbat. If a pagan holiday is nearing, making small steps toward it could be a great daily ritual. Research what you need to do during that holiday and plan for it.
- Call a pagan friend. Whether you need advice on moving forward with your spiritual journey or need a little boost of confidence, talking to a like-minded person can help you immensely.
- Ground and center yourself. You don't have to do meditation or other mindfulness techniques to ground yourself. It takes

simple actions like quieting your mind, walking barefoot, or touching a tree to take advantage of nature's centering power.
- Learn more about your patron or matron deity. Taking even a few minutes daily to learn about the god or goddess you want to connect with will help you honor them and enrich your relationship.

Appendix: A-Z of the Wheel of the Year

As the seasons turn and the cycles of nature unfold, humans have long celebrated the turning points of the year. From ancient times, pagan and polytheistic cultures throughout Europe marked the solstices, equinoxes, and other significant moments with festivals, feasts, and rituals. These celebrations honor nature's gods and goddesses, acknowledge the seasons' changes, and offer a time for reflection, renewal, and community. While some traditions have been lost over time, many continue to be practiced and adapted by modern pagans and polytheists. This chapter explores a selection of these festivals from across Europe, from the well-known to the more obscure, and discovers the rich tapestry of customs and beliefs making the Wheel of the Year.

1. Alban Arthan (AL-ban AHR-than) - December 20th or 21st

Alban Arthan, known as the winter solstice, is a festival celebrating the Sun's rebirth and the return of light after the darkest day of the year. It is a time when the natural world lies dormant, and people gather to kindle the flame of hope and renewal. Many pagan and polytheistic traditions honor the god or goddess of the Sun, such as the Welsh Mabon, the Irish Lugh, and the Roman Sol Invictus. Alban Arthan is a time for introspection, for letting go of the old and welcoming the new. It is a time to celebrate the joys of family and community, share stories, feasts, and gifts, and honor the spirits of the land and the ancestors who came before us. Some popular customs include lighting candles, decorating trees, and holding bonfires. For many, Alban Arthan is a profound and meaningful festival reminding them of the beauty and resilience of the human spirit in the face of darkness.

2. Alban Eilir (AL-ban EYE-leer) - March 20th or 21st

The festival of Alban Eilir, pronounced AL-ban EYE-leer, is celebrated on either March 20th or 21st, marking the arrival of the spring equinox. This ancient pagan festival celebrates the emergence of the natural world from the depths of winter as the earth awakens and new life flourishes. It is a time of balance, when the day and night are equal, and the promise of longer, warmer days are just around the corner. Alban Eilir is honored by many polytheistic traditions, with many cultures offering their own interpretation of the festival. From the Celtic goddess Brigid to the Germanic goddess Ostara and the Greek goddess Persephone, Alban Eilir represents the triumph of fertility and growth over the darkness and cold of winter. The festival is a time to set intentions, plant new seeds, and embrace the renewal of the natural world. It is a time to reconnect with nature, breathe in the fresh air, and revel in the beauty of the world around you. During this festival, people decorate eggs, clean their homes, and engage in other symbolic acts to commemorate the occasion.

3. Brigid (BREE-jid) - February 1st or 2nd

Brigid is a Celtic goddess representing inspiration, creativity, and healing. Her festival is celebrated on February 1st or 2nd, marking the beginning of spring in the Celtic calendar. Brigid is associated with the sacred flame, and her festival is often marked by lighting candles and bonfires. The festival is known as Imbolc, meaning "in the belly" in Old Irish. It represents the time of year when the first stirrings of new life can be felt beneath the earth's surface. In Ireland, Brigid is revered as a patron saint, and her festival is celebrated as St. Brigid's Day, with traditions like making Brigid's crosses and leaving out offerings of milk and bread for her. Across Europe, Brigid's festival is a time for purification and renewal and honoring the divine feminine and the power of nature.

4. Cerealia - April 12th-19th

The Cerealia was an ancient Roman festival celebrated in honor of the goddess Ceres, the goddess of agriculture and grain. The festival was held annually from April 12th to April 19th and was one of the most important celebrations of the Roman calendar. During the Cerealia, the

Romans would honor Ceres by offering milk and honey as well as having processions and conducting various rituals. In ancient times, the Cerealia was a time for farmers to celebrate the arrival of spring and the beginning of the agricultural season. It was a time to give thanks to Ceres for the bounty of the land and ask for her continued blessings throughout the growing season. The festival allowed people to come together and socialize, enjoy the warm weather, and indulge in food, drink, and entertainment. Today, the Cerealia is no longer celebrated as it once was in ancient Rome. However, the legacy of Ceres lives on in the modern world through many traditions and customs associated with agriculture and the celebration of spring. From planting seeds in the garden to enjoying a delicious meal made with fresh, locally grown produce, the spirit of Ceres can be felt in how people honor the earth and the bounty it provides.

5. Feast of Aphrodite - July 23rd

The Feast of Aphrodite falls on July 23rd, celebrating the Greek goddess of love, beauty, and fertility. This festival is associated with the height of summer and the full bloom of nature, making it an ideal time to honor Aphrodite and seek her blessings for love, fertility, and creative inspiration. In ancient Greece, the Feast of Aphrodite was celebrated with offerings of flowers, honey, incense, music, dancing, and feasting. It was a time for lovers to express their devotion to one another and for unmarried women to seek Aphrodite's guidance in finding a suitable partner. Today, modern practitioners of Hellenic Paganism and other traditions honoring the Greek gods and goddesses continue to celebrate the Feast of Aphrodite. This festival is a time for rituals of love and fertility and artistic and creative endeavors. Celebrations include offerings of flowers and honey, dancing, and reading poetry or love spells.

6. Feast of Hekate - November 16th

On November 16th, pagan communities worldwide celebrate the Feast of Hekate, a festival dedicated to the Greek goddess of magic, witchcraft, and the crossroads. Traditionally, this festival was observed with offerings of food, incense, and other gifts at crossroads and other liminal spaces, where Hekate was believed to be most present. It was a time for performing magic and divination and seeking Hekate's guidance in matters of life and death. Modern practitioners of Hellenic Paganism and other traditions honoring Hekate continue to celebrate the Feast of

Hekate. The celebrations include lighting candles, casting spells, and offering food, incense, and other gifts. This festival is a time for reconnecting with the divine and seeking magical blessings for the year ahead. The Feast of Hekate holds special significance for those honoring the goddess of magic and witchcraft. The liminal spaces associated with Hekate represent the crossroads between the physical and spiritual worlds, and the festival offers an opportunity to explore this concept further through ritual and magic.

7. Harvest Home - September 21st or 22nd

As the days grow shorter and the nights longer, the Harvest Home festival marks the end of summer and the beginning of autumn. Celebrated on September 21st or 22nd, it is a time of gratitude for the bountiful harvest that sustains through the long winter months. The Harvest Home festival was a time of feasting and revelry in ancient times, as communities came together to share the fruits of their labor. It was a time for singing, dancing, and telling stories around the fire as the earth turned inward and the leaves began to fall. Today, the Harvest Home festival is celebrated in many parts of Europe, with traditional customs, like crowning a Harvest Queen, decorating the village with boughs of wheat and corn, and blessing the crops. It is a time to give thanks for the earth's abundance and to honor the hard work of farmers and growers who provide food throughout the year.

8. Krampusnacht (KRAHM-pus-nahkt) - December 5th

Krampusnacht, celebrated on December 5th, is a festival with a darker edge. While many associate the winter holiday season with warmth, love, and light, Krampusnacht is a time when fear and mischief take center stage. Originating in Alpine regions of Europe, Krampusnacht is named after Krampus, a horned, demonic creature said to punish naughty children while his benevolent counterpart, St. Nicholas, rewards the good. In many towns and villages, revelers dress up as Krampus and parade through the streets, terrifying young and old with their gruesome costumes and playful pranks. Despite its macabre tone, Krampusnacht is a beloved tradition in many parts of Europe. It is a way to balance light and dark and good and evil. It is a reminder that there is always a balance to be struck in life.

9. Lupercalia (loo-per-KAY-lee-ah) - February 13th-15th

Lupercalia, a festive celebration tracing its roots to ancient Rome, is a time to honor the god of fertility and protect the city from evil spirits.

The festival, held from February 13th to 15th, was dedicated to the god Lupercus and was essential to the city's cultural identity. The priests would wear animal skins, and women were whipped with strips of hide to ensure their fertility and protect them from evil. The festival's association with the founding of Rome adds to its historical significance. The sacrifice of goats and dogs made it a somber event. While Lupercalia is no longer celebrated in its original form, it remains a meaningful time for modern pagans and Wiccans. They have adapted the festival to celebrate the coming of spring and to honor the god of fertility. Nowadays, Lupercalia is a time of feasting, during which participants share food and drink and partake in rituals to welcome the change of season. The spirit of Lupercalia lives on in the modern world as a time when people connect with nature and each other. It is a time to celebrate life and recognize the importance of fertility and growth.

10. Midsummer - June 21st

Midsummer, known as Litha or the Summer Solstice, is a time when the Sun is at its highest point in the sky and the day is the longest. It's celebrated in various ways throughout Europe, with bonfires a common element in many cultures. For example, in Sweden, Midsummer is one of the biggest holidays, and people gather around a maypole to sing and dance traditional folk songs. In other parts of Europe, herbs and flowers are gathered for various magical rituals. It's a time for celebrating the earth's abundance and giving thanks for the harvest to come. The Midsummer celebration is a reminder of the natural world's power and beauty and the importance of living harmoniously with it.

11. Panathenaia (pan-ath-uh-NAY-uh) - July 28th

The Panathenaia, celebrated on July 28th, is a festival dedicated to the Greek goddess Athena, the patron goddess of Athens. It was one of ancient Athens's most important religious festivals and was celebrated every four years. The festival began with a procession through the city, culminating in a grand sacrifice of 100 oxen to the goddess. The festival included athletic and musical competitions and dramatic performances in the Theatre of Dionysus. Panathenaia was a time for Athenians to come together and celebrate their culture and heritage, and it remains a significant cultural event in modern Greece. In modern times, the Panathenaia is still celebrated in Athens and other parts of Greece. The festival retains many traditional elements, such as the procession and the athletic and musical competitions. However, modern celebrations include more contemporary events, such as fireworks displays, concerts, and cultural exhibitions. The festival is an important time for Greeks to celebrate their cultural heritage and unite in a spirit of unity and national pride.

12. Perchtenlauf (PERK-ten-louf) - January 5th or 6th

Perchtenlauf, known as the "Night of the Witches," is a winter festival celebrated in Austria and other parts of Europe on January 5th or 6th. The festival is believed to have its roots in pagan traditions and is dedicated to the goddess Perchta, who roamed the Earth during the winter months. During the festival, men dress in elaborate costumes and masks, representing the Perchten, or "wild spirits." They roam the streets, making noise with bells and wooden sticks to drive away evil spirits and welcome the new year. The festival includes bonfires, feasting, and traditional dance performances. The Perchtenlauf is a time for communities to come together, celebrate their traditions, and banish the darkness of winter with the light of hope and renewal. Today, the festival remains a cherished part of Austrian and European culture, with many communities preserving its ancient customs and adding their unique touches to the celebration.

13. Veneralia (ven-ur-AY-lee-uh) - April 1st

On April 1st, the ancient Romans celebrated Veneralia, a festival dedicated to Venus, the goddess of love and beauty. Veneralia was a time for people to honor and appease the goddess, hoping for her blessings and protection in love and fertility. The festival was marked by offering flowers and incense at Venus' temples and shrines and the ritual washing of her statues. In some parts of Rome, young girls would gather at Venus' temple to ask for her favor in finding a husband, while married women would pray for the health and prosperity of their marriages. Veneralia was a time of great joy and celebration, marked by feasting, drinking, and music. Today, the festival is largely forgotten, but its influence can still be seen in the modern celebration of April Fool's Day, which falls on the same date.

14. Walpurgis Night (WAL-pur-gis nahyt) - April 30th

On the eve of May Day, witches and revelers gather to celebrate Walpurgis Night, a festival with deep roots in pagan tradition. Named after Saint Walpurga, an eighth-century abbess renowned for her healing powers, the festival marks the arrival of spring and the awakening of nature's fertility. In many parts of Europe, people light bonfires, dance around Maypoles, and engage in other traditional rituals to welcome the season of growth and renewal. But Walpurgis Night also has a darker side, as it is said to be a time when the veil between the living and the dead is the thinnest. According to legend, witches and other supernatural beings come out and wreak havoc on unsuspecting villagers. Despite this, the festival remains a time for joy and merriment, as people gather with friends and family to celebrate the arrival of spring and honor their ancestors' traditions.

The world is full of fascinating and diverse pagan and polytheistic festivals celebrated for centuries. From the joyful harvest celebrations to the solemn rites of honoring the dead, these festivals offer a glimpse into ancient cultures' rich and complex beliefs. While many of these traditions have faded over time, some continue to be celebrated in modern times, connecting to the collective past and celebrating cultural heritage. These festivals are a reminder of the power of community, the importance of tradition, and the enduring human need to connect with something greater than self.

Conclusion

As this book has shown, Paganism is an umbrella term for several closely related religions. European Paganism practitioners share the same core beliefs, from the reverence of nature to the universal acceptance of polytheism. They view life as a cycle, similar to nature, which changes with the seasons. It is born, dies, and is revived as a human soul can be reincarnated or live on in the spiritual world. The latter refers to ancestral spirits, significant in Paganism as deities. Ancestors and spirit guides can be summoned for guidance, healing, and protection. The pagan gods and goddesses are typically associated with one aspect of life, although many pagans have deities who embody different aspects and more than one face or name. Several parts of pagan practices are linked to heavenly bodies, with the Sun and the Moon referenced in many myths, legends, and traditions.

This book has explored how the key points of the pagan belief system were incorporated into the various forms of European Paganism, including Celtic Paganism and Druidry, Asatru and Norse Paganism, Germanic Paganism, Slavic Paganism, Greek Polytheism, and Wicca. Naturally, since some of these religions are older than others, there are often wide variations of traditions, even customs related to the same practices or entities. The gods and goddesses have different names and associations and might even be honored through different rituals and ceremonies. However, since the older religions have only survived through oral traditions, their diversified evolution is only comparable to the development of the newer ones to some extent.

Hopefully, the relevant chapters have given you sufficient insight to pique your interest and decide which pagan path to follow. If yes, the last chapter should help you incorporate your chosen path into your life. If you have yet to determine your course, incorporating elements of Paganism into your schedule will help you to get in touch with your spirituality. Remember, Paganism is a highly spiritual and personal practice. While it is beneficial for pagans to share their ideas and rely on like-minded people, you can't forget that your power lies within you. Even little pagan rituals like walking in nature, meditating for 10 minutes, or reciting a prayer to a deity to which you feel drawn can help you find your path and purpose. If you wish to delve deeper into a specific practice and celebrate pagan holidays, refer to this book's Witches Wheel of the Year. It will help you find those that fit your path, needs, and preferences.

Here's another book by Mari Silva that you might like

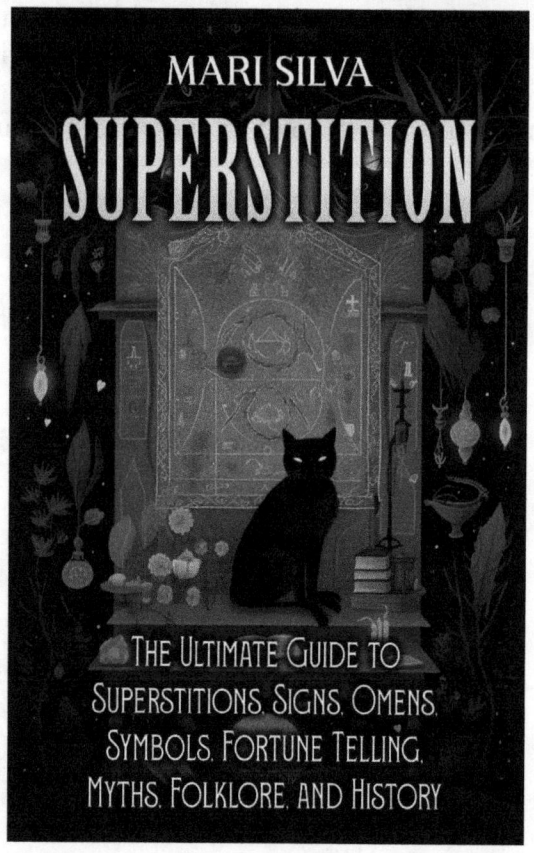

Your Free Gift
(only available for a limited time)

Thanks for getting this book! If you want to learn more about various spirituality topics, then join Mari Silva's community and get a free guided meditation MP3 for awakening your third eye. This guided meditation mp3 is designed to open and strengthen ones third eye so you can experience a higher state of consciousness. Simply visit the link below the image to get started.

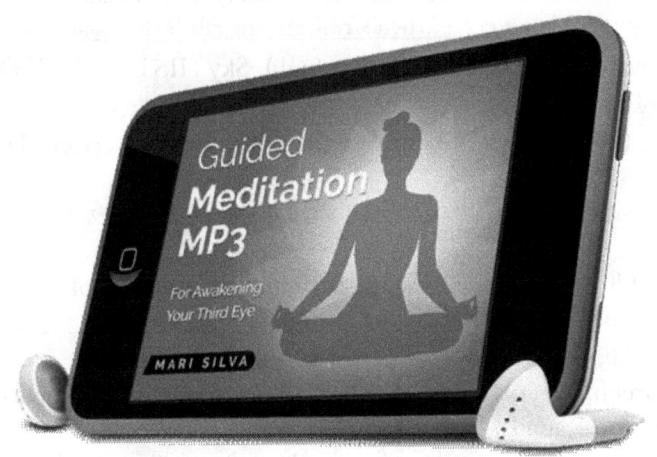

https://spiritualityspot.com/meditation

References

'Celtic' reconstructionism? (n.d.). Tairis.co.uk.

5 obscure pagan festivals around the world. (n.d.). Lonely Planet. https://www.lonelyplanet.com/articles/obscure-pagan-festivals-around-the-world

6 pagan festivals we still celebrate today. (n.d.). Sky HISTORY TV Channel. https://www.history.co.uk/articles/6-pagan-festivals-we-still-celebrate-today

Aburrow, Y. (2015, May 20). Paganism for Beginners – Overview. Dowsing for Divinity. https://www.patheos.com/blogs/sermonsfromthemound/2015/05/paganism-for-beginners1/

Adhikari, S. (2017, November 22). Top 10 important events of Ancient Greece. Ancient History Lists. https://www.ancienthistorylists.com/greek-history/top-10-important-events-of-ancient-greece/

Aldhouse-Green, M. (2015, March 13). The Celtic myths: A guide to the ancient gods and legends. Irish Times. https://www.irishtimes.com/culture/books/the-celtic-myths-a-guide-to-the-ancient-gods-and-legends-1.2136919

Annwfn –. (n.d.). British Fairies. https://britishfairies.wordpress.com/tag/annwfn/

Ásatrú. (2011, April 30). Religion Stylebook. https://religionstylebook.com/entries/asatru

BBC - wales - education - Iron Age Celts - factfile. (n.d.). BBC. https://www.bbc.co.uk/wales/celts/factfile/religion.shtml

Bealtaine rituals to celebrate the May festival. (2021, May 1). Hilda Carroll Holistic Interiors. https://www.hildacarroll.com/bealtaine-beltane/

Being Pagan; Being of the Land: Ecospirituality and Earth-Based Activities among Contemporary Pagans: Weave of reverence: Ritualizing Ecological Practice at Pagan Nature Sanctuaries. (n.d.). Harvard.edu. https://hds.harvard.edu/publications/being-pagan-being-land-ecospirituality-and-earth-based-activities-among-0

Beltane. (2015, August 12). By Land, Sea and Sky. https://thenewpagan.wordpress.com/beltane/

Berry, L. A. (2023, March 15). Who were the Druids? A history of Druidism in Britain. British Heritage. https://britishheritage.com/history/history-druids-britain

Broome, R. (2015, October 30). The story of Ceridwen. Ceridwencentre.co.uk; Ceridwen Centre. https://ceridwencentre.co.uk/the-story-of-ceridwen/

Cartwright, M. (2021a). Ancient Celtic religion. World History Encyclopedia. https://www.worldhistory.org/Ancient_Celtic_Religion/

Cartwright, M. (2021b). Lugh. World History Encyclopedia. https://www.worldhistory.org/Lugh/

Celtic gods. (n.d.). Mythopedia. https://mythopedia.com/topics/celtic-gods

Celtic religion - The Celtic gods. (n.d.). In Encyclopedia Britannica.

Celtic religion. (2022, July 3). Roman Britain. https://www.roman-britain.co.uk/the-celts-and-celtic-life/celtic-religion/

Clan of the entangled thicket 1734. (n.d.). Blogspot.com. http://clanoftheentangledthicket.blogspot.com/2015/12/the-prediu-annwn-exploration.html

Cody. (2011, December 17). What is paganism? Pagan Federation International. https://www.paganfederation.org/what-is-paganism/

Colagrossi, M. (2018, November 27). 10 of the greatest ancient and pagan holidays. Big Think. https://bigthink.com/the-past/pagan-holidays/

Colcombe, R. (2013, July 24). The evolution of the Cauldron into a grail in Celtic Mythology. I. M. H. O. https://medium.com/i-m-h-o/the-evolution-of-the-cauldron-into-a-grail-in-celtic-mythology-a96a41604e9f

Cove, C. (2018, February 21). The whole interesting history of the Tuatha de Danann: Ireland's most ancient race. ConnollyCove. https://www.connollycove.com/tuatha-de-danann/

Dagda. (n.d.). Mythopedia. https://mythopedia.com/topics/dagda

Duffy, K. (2000). Who were the Celts? Barnes & Noble.

Eilenstein, H. (2018). Cernunnos: Vom Schamanen zum Druiden Merlin. Books on Demand.

Festivals and celebrations - RE:ONLINE. (2019, April 18). RE:ONLINE. https://www.reonline.org.uk/knowledge/paganism/festivals-and-celebrations/

Festivals and celebrations - RE:ONLINE. (2019, April 18). RE:ONLINE.
https://www.reonline.org.uk/knowledge/paganism/festivals-and-celebrations/

Fields, K. (2018, October 14). Daily Pagan Rituals: List of 30+ SIMPLE Everyday Traditions. Otherworldly Oracle.
https://otherworldlyoracle.com/simple-daily-pagan-rituals/

Germanic paganism. (n.d.). Religion Wiki.
https://religion.fandom.com/wiki/Germanic_paganism

Germanic religion and mythology - Mythology. (n.d.). In Encyclopedia Britannica

Hart, A. (n.d.). How To Find Your Patron Deity & If You Should Even Bother. The Traveling Witch. https://thetravelingwitch.com/blog/how-to-find-your-patron-deity-if-you-should-even-bother

Hellenism. (n.d.). Paganfed.org. https://www.paganfed.org/hellenism/

Hemingway, C. (1 C.E., January 1). Greek gods and religious practices. The Met's Heilbrunn Timeline of Art History.
https://www.metmuseum.org/toah/hd/grlg/hd_grlg.htm

How can I find and connect with others pagans, wiccans, and witches in my area? (n.d.). Quora. https://www.quora.com/How-can-I-find-and-connect-with-others-pagans-wiccans-and-witches-in-my-area

Jarus, O. (2022, September 23). The mysterious history of druids, ancient "mediators between humans and the gods." Livescience.com; Live Science.
https://www.livescience.com/who-were-the-druids

JustCode. (n.d.). Creidhne - God of Metalworkers. - Irish God. Thewhitegoddess.co.uk.
http://www.thewhitegoddess.co.uk/divinity_of_the_day/irish/creidhne.asp

King Arthur the voyager - by Katherine Langrish. (n.d.). Blogspot.com.
http://the-history-girls.blogspot.com/2014/12/king-arthur-voyager-by-katherine.html

Langrish, K. (2016). Seven Miles of steel thistles: Essays on fairy tales. Greystones Press.

Litha / Midsummer. (2015, August 9). By Land, Sea and Sky.
https://thenewpagan.wordpress.com/midsummer-litha/

Lugh. (n.d.). Mythopedia. https://mythopedia.com/topics/lugh

Lughnasadh / Lammas. (2015, August 9). By Land, Sea and Sky.
https://thenewpagan.wordpress.com/lughnasadh-lammas/

Mabon / autumn equinox. (2015, September 3). By Land, Sea and Sky.
https://thenewpagan.wordpress.com/wheel-of-the-year/mabon-autumn-equinox/

McLean, A. P. J. (n.d.). The Germanic Tribes. Lumenlearning.Com. https://courses.lumenlearning.com/atd-herkimer-westerncivilization/chapter/the-germanic-tribes/

Meet the Slavs. (2020, November 7). Slavic Magic: Rituals, Spells, and Herbs. Meet the Slavs. https://meettheslavs.com/slavic-magic/

Meet the Slavs. (2021, July 13). Slavic Paganism: History and Rituals. Meet the Slavs. https://meettheslavs.com/slavic-paganism/

Meet the Slavs. (2021, July 5). Top 6 Slavic Pagan Holidays. Meet the Slavs. https://meettheslavs.com/slavic-pagan-holidays/

My hellenismos 101. (n.d.). Hellenion.org. https://www.hellenion.org/essays-on-hellenic-polytheism/my-hellenismos-101/

Neal, C. F. (2015). Imbolc: Rituals, recipes and lore for Brigid's day. Llewellyn Publications.

No title. (n.d.-a). Study.com. https://study.com/academy/lesson/celtic-paganism-history-deities-facts-ancient-religion.html

No title. (n.d.-b). Study.com. https://study.com/learn/lesson/pantheism-religions-and-beliefs.html

O'Hara, K. (2023, January 2). The Morrigan: The story of the fiercest goddess in Irish myth. The Irish Road Trip. https://www.theirishroadtrip.com/the-morrigan/

Oertel, K. (Ed.). (2015). Ásatrú: Die Rückkehr der Götter (3rd ed.). Edition Roter Drache.

Ostara / spring equinox. (2015, August 16). By Land, Sea and Sky. https://thenewpagan.wordpress.com/ostara-spring-equinox/

Rajchel, D. (2015). Samhain: Rituals, Recipes & Lore for Halloween. Llewellyn Publications. https://thenewpagan.wordpress.com/wheel-of-the-year/samhain/

Rune, S. (2015). Paganism: The ultimate guide to paganism, inlcuding Wicca, spirituality, spells & practises for a pagan life. Createspace Independent Publishing Platform.

Sacred texts: Wicca and Neo-Paganism. (n.d.). Sacred-texts.com. https://www.sacred-texts.com/pag/

slife. (2020, June 10). Germanic Paganism. The Spiritual Life. https://slife.org/germanic-paganism/

Smith, D. (2016, March 26). Wiccan holidays: Celebrating the sun on the Sabbats. Dummies. https://www.dummies.com/article/body-mind-spirit/religion-spirituality/wicca/wiccan-holidays-celebrating-the-sun-on-the-sabbats-192774/

Sunshine, G. (2020, February 4). Wicca and eclectic Neo-Paganism: Beliefs and practices, emerging worldviews 22. Breakpoint.

https://breakpoint.org/wicca-and-eclectic-neo-paganism-beliefs-and-practices-emerging-worldviews-22/

The Absolute Basics Paganism. (n.d.). Umass.edu. https://www.umass.edu/rso/spirals/Site/Paganism_101.html

The Current Chief, The Former Chief, & Patroness, O. (2019a, November 27). Druid beliefs. Order of Bards, Ovates & Druids; OBOD. https://druidry.org/druid-way/beliefs

The Current Chief, The Former Chief, & Patroness, O. (2019b, November 27). History of the druids. Order of Bards, Ovates & Druids; OBOD. https://druidry.org/druid-way/what-druidry/a-longer-history

The Hellenistic period-cultural & historical overview. (2018, June 14). Department of Classics. https://www.colorado.edu/classics/2018/06/14/hellenistic-period-cultural-historical-overview

The old Nordic religion today. (n.d.). National Museum of Denmark. https://en.natmus.dk/historical-knowledge/denmark/prehistoric-period-until-1050-ad/the-viking-age/religion-magic-death-and-rituals/the-old-nordic-religion-today/

The Pagan year. (n.d.). BBC. https://www.bbc.co.uk/religion/religions/paganism/holydays/year.shtml

The Witch is In. (n.d.). Tumblr. https://herecomesthewitch.tumblr.com/post/157912148899/laurels-guide-to-grimoires

The. (2018, August 10). Neo-paganism offers something old and something new. Economist (London, England: 1843). https://www.economist.com/erasmus/2018/08/10/neo-paganism-offers-something-old-and-something-new

Thomas, P. V. (n.d.). Ancient Celtic Religion. Tutorialspoint.com. https://www.tutorialspoint.com/ancient-celtic-religion

V. (2018). Morrigan. Independently Published.

What is Asatru? (2013, December 4). Gotquestions.org. https://www.gotquestions.org/Asatru.html

Wheel of the Year. (2013, June 22). The Celtic Journey. https://thecelticjourney.wordpress.com/the-celts/wheel-of-the-year/

Wheel of the Year: The 8 Wiccan holiday festivals - Wicca Academy. (n.d.). https://wiccaacademy.com/wheel-of-the-year/

Who were the Druids? (2017, March 21). Historic UK. https://www.historic-uk.com/HistoryUK/HistoryofWales/Druids/

Wigington, P. (2007, August 19). Hellenic Polytheism and the Reconstruction of Greek Paganism. Learn Religions. https://www.learnreligions.com/about-hellenic-polytheism-2562548

Wigington, P. (2007a, June 24). The legend of Lugh, the Celtic craftsman god. Learn Religions. https://www.learnreligions.com/lugh-master-of-skills-2561970

Wigington, P. (2007b, September 19). Brighid, the hearth goddess of Ireland. Learn Religions. https://www.learnreligions.com/brighid-hearth-goddess-of-ireland-2561958

Wigington, P. (2008a, November 2). The Morrighan. Learn Religions. https://www.learnreligions.com/the-morrighan-of-ireland-2561971

Wigington, P. (2008b, December 13). Cernunnos, the wild Celtic god of the Forest. Learn Religions. https://www.learnreligions.com/cernunnos-wild-god-of-the-forest-2561959

Wigington, P. (2009, August 7). Pagan gods and goddesses. Learn Religions. https://www.learnreligions.com/pagan-gods-and-goddesses-2561985

Wigington, P. (2009a, August 4). The Dagda, the father god of Ireland. Learn Religions. https://www.learnreligions.com/the-dagda-father-god-of-ireland-2561706

Wigington, P. (2009b, August 5). 10 Celtic deities you should know. Learn Religions. https://www.learnreligions.com/gods-of-the-celts-2561711

Wigington, P. (2012, June 20). Resources for Celtic pagans. Learn Religions. https://www.learnreligions.com/resources-for-celtic-pagans-2562555

Wigington, P. (n.d.). The 10 Most Important Slavic Gods. ThoughtCo. https://www.thoughtco.com/slavic-gods-4768505

wikiHow. (2011, July 30). How to Set up a Simple Pagan or Wiccan Altar. WikiHow. https://www.wikihow.com/Set-up-a-Simple-Pagan-or-Wiccan-Altar

Wright, M. S. (2013, January 23). Ideas for Celebrating Pagan Holidays With Family and Children. Exemplore. https://exemplore.com/paganism/Imbolc-for-Pagan-Families-Ideas-for-Celebrating-with-Children

Yule / Midwinter. (2015, August 27). By Land, Sea and Sky. https://thenewpagan.wordpress.com/wheel-of-the-year/yule-midwinter/

ztevetevans. (2021, April 30). Celtic lore: Cauldrons – the magical, the mythical and the real. Under the Influence! https://ztevetevans.wordpress.com/2021/04/30/celtic-lore-cauldrons-the-magical-the-mythical-and-the-real

www.ingramcontent.com/pod-product-compliance
Lightning Source LLC
Chambersburg PA
CBHW051846160426
43209CB00006B/1177